THE PARABLES OF JESUS IN THE GOSPELS

BIBLE BASED WISDOM: LIFE LESSONS FOR MODERN DAILY LIVING

Richard Louden

ISBN: 979-8-9920675-0-7 (Hardback)

ISBN: 979-8-9920675-2-1 (Paperback)

ISBN: 979-8-9920675-1-4 (eBook)

This book is lovingly dedicated to my wife, Debbie.

Having read the Bible many times, Debbie always returns to the four Gospels, finding inspiration in the life and teachings of Jesus and his Parables. And even now, as she bravely battles cancer and endures multiple rounds of chemotherapy and other challenging treatments, Debbie maintains a spirit of happiness and compassion. Her resilience and grace inspire all of us to live better lives and follow the lessons of Jesus in the Gospels.

The Parables of Jesus in the Gospels

Contents

PREFACE

The Parables of Jesus in the Gospels offer timeless wisdom for those seeking to lead a fulfilling and purposeful life through faith. This book delves into each Parable, presenting a concise summary followed by two insightful interpretations: one rooted in traditional Christian teachings and another offering added insights into the guidance of the Parable. Furthermore, personal reflections are shared about each Parable inspired by my own life journey and faith experiences.

As you explore the interpretations and personal reflections presented in this book, you may discover new insights that resonate deeply with your faith journey. Each perspective is thoughtfully rooted in biblical teachings, ensuring alignment with traditional Christian beliefs while offering insights to illuminate the timeless relevance of Jesus' Parables. The book aims to inspire meaningful reflection and deepen your connection to the profound lessons found in the Parables of Jesus, supporting spiritual journey and faith.

Moreover, I hope this book can serve as a valuable tool for fostering meaningful discussions with your children or grandchildren about important concepts such as kindness, forgiveness, honesty, ethics, and more.

Enjoy your journey through the Parables, and may they inspire and enlighten you on your path.

INTRODUCTION

In first-century Jewish society (and throughout the broader ancient Near East), storytelling was a common, culturally accepted way to convey moral and spiritual truths. Traveling teachers, rabbis, and philosophers would use short narratives and relatable, everyday examples—much like parables—to capture an audience's attention and illustrate deeper principles in a memorable way. These oral traditions fit particularly well in an era where most people could not read or write, and where strong verbal communication was essential for passing on wisdom.

Thus, Jesus' use of parables was neither unusual nor out of place for His time. What distinguishes His parables is that they have miraculously endured, shaping generations of believers and inquirers while offering vivid lessons on compassion, forgiveness, and faith. Jesus often drew on everyday images—seeds, vineyards, and household items—to convey deeper truths about living a life of integrity, love, and purpose. By looking beyond the ancient setting and recognizing universal themes, we discover that these parables remain remarkably relevant, guiding us toward ethical, meaningful choices in our modern world.

Prior to Jesus' life, in the 13th century BCE, Moses led the Exodus from Egypt and was given the laws of God (the Mosaic Covenant) at Mount Sinai. Jesus' teachings are often compared with these older biblical laws by religious scholars—highlighting how He introduces a new depth of grace and love. I've included an Epilogue at the conclusion of this book for those who wish to learn more about my perspective on how the Old and New Testaments interact. But first, I invite you to immerse yourself in these parables as they are, letting them illuminate your understanding in fresh ways.

It can be said with certainty that Jesus' life stands as the ultimate role model for Christians. Yet I also believe that people of virtually any faith—or even those without a formal faith—can use the Parables to become the best version of themselves. The Parables were a critical part of Jesus' message and role modeling. I invite you to explore these short yet powerful stories to see how they might speak to your own life today.

1. Parable of the Unclean Spirit – Mathew 12 43-45

When the unclean spirit is gone out of a man, he walketh through dry places, seeking rest, and findeth none.

⁴⁴ Then he saith, I will return into my house from whence I came out; and when he is come, he findeth it empty, swept, and garnished.

⁴⁵ Then goeth he, and taketh with himself seven other spirits more wicked than himself, and they enter in and dwell there: and the last state of that man is worse than the first. Even so shall it be also unto this wicked generation.

SUMMARY

The Parable of the Unclean Spirit is a story Jesus told about an evil spirit that left a person. The spirit went to find a new home but did not find one. So, it decided to return to the person it left. When it came back, it found the person's heart clean and tidy. The spirit brought seven other spirits that were even worse, and they all moved in.

INTERPRETATION

The traditional meaning of this parable is that it's not enough to just get rid of something bad in our lives. We also need to replace it fully with love and faith in God. Otherwise, the bad thing might come back, and we could end up in an even worse situation.

An additional insight is that it teaches us about using God's Gift of initiative and positive influences to improve how we live our lives. We should fill our lives with goodness, positive activities and strong positive relationships to truly experience a good and positive life.

PERSONAL THOUGHTS

Alcoholics Anonymous (AA) was founded in the 1930's. Their approach to alcoholism came from personal experiences and trial and error of early members. They found that once the negative influence of alcohol was gone, a void remained—one that could easily draw something even more destructive into their life if left empty.

AA teaches that recovering alcoholics must do more than just stop drinking; they must fill the gap previously occupied by alcohol with positive spiritual growth, moral inventory, and the support of others walking the same path. By embracing a higher power, practicing the Twelve Steps, and nurturing a sense of purpose and community, they "fill the void" with something good, preventing the return of old habits or something worse.

In both Jesus' Parable and the journey of AA, we see that true freedom and lasting change come not merely from removing what harms us, but by intentionally replacing it with faith, accountability, and transformative growth.

2. Parable of the Sower – Mark 4 3-9

[3] Hearken; Behold, there went out a sower to sow:[4] And it came to pass, as he sowed, some fell by the way side, and the fowls of the air came and devoured it up.

[5] And some fell on stony ground, where it had not much earth; and immediately it sprang up, because it had no depth of earth:[6] But when the sun was up, it was scorched; and because it had no root, it withered away.

[7] And some fell among thorns, and the thorns grew up, and choked it, and it yielded no fruit.[8] And other fell on good ground, and did yield fruit that sprang up and increased; and brought forth, some thirty, and some sixty, and some an hundred.

[9] And he said unto them, He that hath ears to hear, let him hear.

Summary

The Parable of the Sower is a story Jesus told about a farmer who went out to plant seeds. Some seeds fell on the path and were eaten by birds, some fell on rocky ground and couldn't grow deep roots, some fell among thorns and got choked by the weeds, but some fell on good soil and grew into healthy plants that produced lots of grain.

Interpretation

The traditional meaning of this parable is that people are like the different types of soil, and the seeds represent God's message. When people hear the message, they react differently. Some don't understand it, some lose faith when life gets hard, some get distracted by other things, but some truly understand and believe in the message, so their lives are changed for the better and they help spread God's message to others.

An additional insight is it teaches us about the importance of being open and receptive to God's teachings. The story reminds us that we should be like the good soil, ready to listen, understand, and accept God's message. When we do this, our lives will be transformed, and we will be able to share the love and wisdom we've gained with others, helping them to grow and flourish as well.

Personal Thoughts

Many years ago, my wife Debbie decided to focus on personal growth. In her daily life, she made it a point to smile at people, offer small compliments, and perform little acts of kindness. Just like the seeds in the parable that fell on the path, rocky ground, and among thorns, she knew that not all her efforts would be appreciated or make a difference. But she also believed that sometimes, these small gestures would brighten someone's day and have a positive ripple effect. She'll never know the full extent of the results of her actions, but taking these steps brings her happiness as well as happiness to others.

3. Parable of the Rich Fool – Luke 12 16-21

And he spake a parable unto them, saying, The ground of a certain rich man brought forth plentifully:

¹⁷ And he thought within himself, saying, What shall I do, because I have no room where to bestow my fruits?

¹⁸ And he said, This will I do: I will pull down my barns, and build greater; and there will I bestow all my fruits and my goods.

¹⁹ And I will say to my soul, Soul, thou hast much goods laid up for many years; take thine ease, eat, drink, and be merry.

²⁰ But God said unto him, Thou fool, this night thy soul shall be required of thee: then whose shall those things be, which thou hast provided?

SUMMARY

The Parable of the Rich Fool is a story Jesus told about a rich man who had a great harvest and decided to build bigger barns to store all his crops and possessions. He thought he had plenty saved up and could relax and enjoy his life. But God told him he was foolish because he would die that very night, and then all his wealth would be useless.

INTERPRETATION

The traditional meaning of this parable is that we should not be focused only on storing treasures and possessions for ourselves. Instead, we should be generous and use our wealth to help others and please God, because life is short, and we never know when our time will come.

An additional insight is that it teaches us about the importance of valuing the things that truly matter in life. The rich man was focused on his wealth and possessions, but he didn't consider his relationships with others or his spiritual well-being. This story reminds us to prioritize love, kindness, and our relationship with God over material possessions because, in the end, those are the things that will truly make our lives meaningful and fulfilling.

PERSONAL THOUGHTS

As the saying goes, "no one on their deathbed ever said they wish they had spent more time at work!" This parable reminds us to prioritize what is truly important in life. These priorities may vary for each of us and could include relationships with others, kindness, forgiveness, charity, or many other meaningful aspects of life. It's a call to reflect on our values and ensure we invest our time and energy in what truly matters.

4. Parable of the Mustard Seed – Mark 4 30-32

And he said, Whereunto shall we liken the kingdom of God? or with what comparison shall we compare it?

[31] It is like a grain of mustard seed, which, when it is sown in the earth, is less than all the seeds that be in the earth:[32] But when it is sown, it groweth up, and becometh greater than all herbs, and shooteth out great branches; so that the fowls of the air may lodge under the shadow of it.

SUMMARY

The Parable of the Mustard Seed is a story Jesus told about a tiny mustard seed that, when planted in the ground, grows into a big tree. Even though the seed is very small, it becomes a large plant where birds can come and rest on its branches.

INTERPRETATION

The traditional meaning of this parable is that something small, like a little bit of faith or a small act of kindness, can grow into something much bigger and make a significant difference in the world. Just like the tiny mustard seed becomes a big tree, our faith can grow and have a positive impact on those around us.

An additional insight is that it shows how the Kingdom of God starts small but eventually grows to be very large. It's a reminder that even though the beginnings may seem small or insignificant, God can use it to create something incredible and life changing. We should never underestimate the power of small actions or the potential for growth in ourselves and others.

PERSONAL THOUGHTS

This parable resonates with me as a symbol of growth and potential. It shows how something small, like a dream or concept, can grow into something significant. When I started this book, it was a small step taken during a challenging time, meant only for the benefit of my wife Debbie and me. Much like the mustard seed, it has now grown beyond my initial expectations and might be helpful and meaningful to many others. This parable inspires us to never underestimate small beginnings, teaching that patience, perseverance, and belief in our potential can lead to significant achievements, just as the tiny mustard seed grows into a large tree.

5. Parable of the Workers in the Vineyard – Mathew 20 1-16

For the kingdom of heaven is like unto a man that is an householder, which went out early in the morning to hire labourers into his vineyard.[2] And when he had agreed with the labourers for a penny a day, he sent them into his vineyard.

[3] And he went out about the third hour, and saw others standing idle in the marketplace,[4] And said unto them; Go ye also into the vineyard, and whatsoever is right I will give you. And they went their way.

[5] Again he went out about the sixth and ninth hour, and did likewise.[6] And about the eleventh hour he went out, and found others standing idle, and saith unto them, Why stand ye here all the day idle?

[7] They say unto him, Because no man hath hired us. He saith unto them, Go ye also into the vineyard; and whatsoever is right, that shall ye receive.[8] So when even was come, the lord of the vineyard saith unto his steward, Call the labourers, and give them their hire, beginning from the last unto the first.

[9] And when they came that were hired about the eleventh hour, they received every man a penny.[10] But when the first came, they supposed that they should have received more; and they likewise received every man a penny.

[11] And when they had received it, they murmured against the good man of the house,[12] Saying, These last have wrought but one hour, and thou hast made them equal unto us, which have borne the burden and heat of the day.

[13] But he answered one of them, and said, Friend, I do thee no wrong: didst not thou agree with me for a penny?[14] Take that thine is, and go thy way: I will give unto this last, even as unto thee.

[15] Is it not lawful for me to do what I will with mine own? Is thine eye evil, because I am good? [16] For the last shall be first and the first last: for many be called but few chosen.

SUMMARY

The Parable of the Workers in the Vineyard is a story Jesus told about a landowner who hired workers to work in his vineyard. He hired some workers early in the morning and agreed to pay them a certain amount for a day's work. Later in the day, he hired more workers, and then even more just an hour before quitting time. When the workday ended, he paid all the workers the same amount, even the ones who had only worked for an hour. The workers who had been there all day were upset because they thought they should get more money. But the landowner explained that he was being generous to the latecomers, and the early workers were still getting the pay they had agreed to.

INTERPRETATION

The traditional meaning of this parable is that God's love and generosity are not limited by how long we have been following Him. Even if we start following God's teachings later in life, we are still just as important and valuable to Him as those who have been following Him for a long time. This story reminds us not to be jealous or resentful of others, but to be grateful for God's love and kindness.

An additional insight of this parable is that it teaches us about fairness and generosity. The landowner in the story showed kindness to the latecomers, even though they hadn't worked as long. This story encourages us to be generous in our dealings with others, and not to judge people based on how much they have done, but rather on their willingness to participate and contribute.

PERSONAL THOUGHTS

When I compare my accomplishments and compensation to my peers, or when my friends compare theirs to their coworkers, it often leads to stress and dissatisfaction rather than anything constructive. This parable teaches us to appreciate what we have instead of being resentful or envious of others, regardless of how we perceive the fairness of life. As many people I know have told their kids, "Life is not fair, deal with it!" Embracing this lesson can help us focus on our own blessings and contributions, fostering a more positive and contented outlook.

6 PARABLE OF THE HIDDEN TREASURE – MATHEW 13 44

Again, the kingdom of heaven is like unto treasure hid in a field; the which when a man hath found, he hideth, and for joy thereof goeth and selleth all that he hath, and buyeth that field.

SUMMARY

The Parable of the Hidden Treasure is a story Jesus told about a man who found a treasure buried in a field. He was so excited about his discovery that he hid the treasure again, sold everything he owned, and bought the field so he could have the treasure forever.

INTERPRETATION

The traditional meaning of this parable is that discovering the Kingdom of God is like finding a hidden treasure. When we understand how valuable it is, we should be willing to give up everything else to be part of it, because it's worth more than anything we have.

An additional insight is that it shows how important it is to be focused on what truly matters in life. The man in the story realized the value of the treasure and was willing to make sacrifices to gain it. Similarly, we should prioritize our relationship with God and be willing to let go of things that might hold us back from fully experiencing the joy and peace that come from knowing Him.

PERSONAL THOUGHTS

For me, this parable is thought-provoking because it doesn't mention the man sharing the treasure, which represents his finding of the kingdom of God. Perhaps it suggests that not everyone is called to the same roles in life or to be evangelicals. Some of us might not have the natural ability to spread the word without risking alienating others. In such cases, we can cherish our own faith and focus on living a good and positive life, serving as role models whom others can respect and learn from.

7. Parable of the Wicket Tenants – Mark 12 1-12

And he began to speak unto them by parables. A certain man planted a vineyard, and set an hedge about it, and digged a place for the winefat, and built a tower, and let it out to husbandmen, and went into a far country.

² And at the season he sent to the husbandmen a servant, that he might receive from the husbandmen of the fruit of the vineyard.

³ And they caught him, and beat him, and sent him away empty. ⁴ And again he sent unto them another servant; and at him they cast stones, and wounded him in the head, and sent him away shamefully handled.

⁵ And again he sent another; and him they killed, and many others; beating some, and killing some. ⁶ Having yet therefore one son, his wellbeloved, he sent him also last unto them, saying, They will reverence my son.

⁷ But those husbandmen said among themselves, This is the heir; come, let us kill him, and the inheritance shall be our›s. ⁸ And they took him, and killed him, and cast him out of the vineyard.

⁹ What shall therefore the lord of the vineyard do? he will come and destroy the husbandmen, and will give the vineyard unto others. ¹⁰ And have ye not read this scripture; The stone which the builders rejected is become the head of the corner:

¹¹ This was the Lord›s doing, and it is marvellous in our eyes? ¹² And they sought to lay hold on him, but feared the people: for they knew that he had spoken the parable against them: and they left him, and went their way.

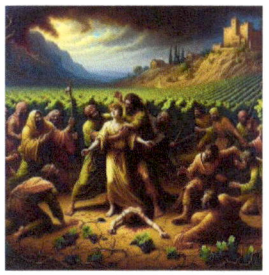

SUMMARY

The Parable of the Wicked Tenants is a story Jesus told about a landowner who rented his vineyard to some tenants. When it was time to collect the fruits, the landowner sent his servants to the tenants. But the tenants mistreated the servants, beating some and even killing others. The landowner then sent his own son, thinking the tenants would respect him. But the tenants killed the son too, hoping to take his inheritance. When the owner hears about this, he comes and punishes the wicked tenants and gives the vineyard to others who will give him his share of the fruit at the harvest time.

INTERPRETATION

The traditional meaning of this parable is that the tenants represent the people who reject God's message and mistreat His messengers. The landowner's son represents Jesus, who was sent by God but was rejected and killed by the people. This story teaches us the importance of listening to and respecting God's message, and not to be like the wicked tenants who rejected and harmed the messengers.

An additional insight is that it teaches us about the consequences of our actions. The wicked tenants in the story made bad choices, and as a result, they faced punishment from the landowner. This story reminds us that we should choose to do good and treat others with kindness and respect, because our actions have consequences and can impact not only our own lives but also the lives of others.

PERSONAL THOUGHTS

Some years ago, we rented out a couple of houses. One tenant, a very responsible woman, took loving care of the house and always paid rent on time. One day, she asked if she could move to our other house, which had a lower rent and was available at the time. Although we appreciated her reliability as a tenant in the higher-rent house, we agreed to let her move into the cheaper house. Since she had been an outstanding tenant, we wanted to help her out and keep her as a long-term tenant. This personal experience shows that being a good tenant and a reliable person can lead to additional benefits and long-term opportunities. It reminds us of the importance of being trustworthy and responsible in all our dealings.

8. Parable of the Dragnet – Mathew 13 47-50

Again, the kingdom of heaven is like unto a net, that was cast into the sea, and gathered of every kind:

[48] Which, when it was full, they drew to shore, and sat down, and gathered the good into vessels, but cast the bad away.

[49] So shall it be at the end of the world: the angels shall come forth, and sever the wicked from among the just,

[50] And shall cast them into the furnace of fire: there shall be wailing and gnashing of teeth.

SUMMARY

The Parable of the Dragnet is a story about fishermen who threw a big net into the sea to catch fish. When they pulled the net back up, it was full of all kinds of fish. They sorted the fish, keeping the good ones and throwing the bad ones away.

INTERPRETATION

The traditional meaning of this parable is that at the end of time, God will sort people just like the fishermen sorted the fish. The good people will be kept in God's kingdom, while the bad ones will be thrown away.

An additional insight is that it teaches us about the importance of living a good life. Just like the fishermen sorted the fish, we should strive to be good and make positive choices so that we can be part of God's kingdom when the time comes.

PERSONAL THOUGHTS

In our journey through life, we encounter a multitude of experiences, people, and ideas; much like a net that captures various kinds of fish. We can learn from these experiences and choose to keep what makes us better individuals. My job took our family to many cities in the U.S., as well as to Pakistan and Indonesia. Through these travels, we saw many sides of different people, cultures, and religions, gaining an understanding of life and the world we could never have achieved otherwise. We had both good and bad experiences wherever we went. We learned that there are good people everywhere and that stereotypes are rarely accurate. This parable reminds us of the importance of being open to life's diverse offerings and not being afraid to cast our personal net far and wide, keeping the new knowledge, positive role models, and cherished memories with us always.

9. PARABLE OF THE LOST SHEEP - LUKE 15 3-7

And he spake this parable unto them, saying,

[4] What man of you, having an hundred sheep, if he lose one of them, doth not leave the ninety and nine in the wilderness, and go after that which is lost, until he find it?[5] And when he hath found it, he layeth it on his shoulders, rejoicing.

[6] And when he cometh home, he calleth together his friends and neighbours, saying unto them, Rejoice with me; for I have found my sheep which was lost.[7] I say unto you, that likewise joy shall be in heaven over one sinner that repenteth, more than over ninety and nine just persons, which need no repentance.

SUMMARY

The Parable of the Lost Sheep is a story Jesus told about a shepherd who had 100 sheep. One day, one of the sheep got lost. Instead of just staying with the 99 sheep that were safe, the shepherd went out to look for the lost one. When he finally found it, he was so happy that he carried it back to the flock on his shoulders and celebrated with his friends.

INTERPRETATION

The traditional meaning of this parable is that God loves each and every one of us, just like the shepherd loves all his sheep. Even if we make mistakes or feel lost, God will always look for us and welcome us back with open arms. This story reminds us that no matter what, God cares for us and wants us to return to Him when we're lost.

An additional insight of this parable is that it teaches us about the importance of caring for others. Just like the shepherd didn't give up on the lost sheep, we should also be willing to help and support people who might be lost or struggling in life. This story encourages us to show kindness, compassion, and understanding to everyone, because every person is valuable and deserves to be cared for.

PERSONAL THOUGHTS

Debbie had a friend in high school who was quiet and had few friends. She never married and never had much money. A few times a year, Debbie would reach out to her, and they would exchange greetings. Occasionally, if passing through her town, Debbie would visit her. Around the age of 50, Debbie realized they hadn't been in touch for a few years. When she contacted her friend, she discovered that her friend had lost her job and had been out of work for many months. Debbie decided to make the trip to visit her and found that her friend had no surviving relatives, her car was no longer working, and her house was literally falling apart. Debbie chose to help her friend by finding a job near us, covering the moving costs and apartment deposit. Debbie was always thankful she had made the effort to check on her friend. This story reminds me of this parable, showing the importance of reaching out and caring for those who might be struggling and feeling lost.

10. Parable of the Watchful Servants – Luke 12 35-40

Let your loins be girded about, and your lights burning;

[36] And ye yourselves like unto men that wait for their lord, when he will return from the wedding; that when he cometh and knocketh, they may open unto him immediately.

[37] Blessed are those servants, whom the lord when he cometh shall find watching: verily I say unto you, that he shall gird himself, and make them to sit down to meat, and will come forth and serve them.[38] And if he shall come in the second watch, or come in the third watch, and find them so, blessed are those servants.

[39] And this know, that if the goodman of the house had known what hour the thief would come, he would have watched, and not have suffered his house to be broken through.[40] Be ye therefore ready also: for the Son of man cometh at an hour when ye think not.

Summary

The Parable of the Watchful Servants is a story Jesus told about servants who were waiting for their master to return home from a wedding. They didn't know exactly when he would come back, but they stayed awake and ready so they could open the door for him as soon as he arrived. When the master returned, he was pleased to find the servants awake and prepared, and he rewarded them.

Interpretation

The traditional meaning of this parable is that we should always be ready and watchful for Jesus' return. We don't know when it will happen, but we should live our lives in a way that we are prepared and doing what God wants us to always do.

An additional insight is that it teaches us about the importance of being responsible and doing our best in everything we do. The watchful servants were alert and prepared, showing that they took their duties seriously. This story reminds us to stay focused and committed to the tasks we have been given, whether they are big or small, because our dedication and hard work will be noticed and appreciated.

Personal Thoughts

Debbie and I retired to a small ranch in Louisiana. Carlos works for us there 1½ days a week. We travel a lot and are often gone for weeks at a time. Occasionally, we return from a trip earlier than planned, but we always find Carlos diligently working, whether we are there or not. We greatly admire him for his dedication, and he has become irreplaceable to us.

Because he is so honest and trustworthy, we are thankful to have Carlos as both a friend and an employee, and we reward him for that. Whenever he needs a day off, a schedule change, or any favor, we are happy to grant it. We will always take care of him, as he has always been loyal to us. This parable reminds us of the value of being reliable and diligent, and how such qualities are appreciated and rewarded.

11. Parable of the Salt and Light – Mathew 5 13-16

Ye are the salt of the earth: but if the salt have lost his savour, wherewith shall it be salted? it is thenceforth good for nothing, but to be cast out, and to be trodden under foot of men.

[14] Ye are the light of the world. A city that is set on an hill cannot be hid.

[15] Neither do men light a candle, and put it under a bushel, but on a candlestick; and it giveth light unto all that are in the house.

[16] Let your light so shine before men, that they may see your good works, and glorify your Father which is in heaven.

SUMMARY

The Parable of the Salt and Light is a teaching from Jesus where he compared his followers to salt and light. He said that if salt loses its flavor, it's not useful anymore, and if a light is hidden, it won't help anyone see in the dark. So, just like salt and light, his followers should make a positive difference in the world and let their good actions shine for others to see.

INTERPRETATION

The traditional meaning of this parable is that as followers of Jesus, we should live our lives in a way that helps and inspires others. We should be like salt, making things better, and like light, guiding others in the right direction.

An additional insight is that it teaches us about the importance of being true to ourselves and our beliefs. If we lose our "flavor" or hide our "light," we're not living up to our full potential. This story reminds us that we should always strive to be the best version of ourselves and to let our actions and values positively influence those around us.

PERSONAL THOUGHTS

Debbie's uncle was a Baptist preacher and a good man. One day, I went with him and a family group to a busy restaurant. He immediately spoke up, asked everyone at our table to hold hands, bow their heads, and he said a prayer in the noisy restaurant. It felt uncomfortable to me, given my personal trait of being embarrassed calling attention to myself. I also know some people would consider this grandstanding or pretentious and believe a subtle, individual silent prayer is more appropriate. His intentions were surely guided by the Parable of the Salt and the Light. He wanted to shine a light on giving thanks before each meal.

Personally, I believe how we interpret the Gospels and become our best Christian selves may be unique to each of us depending on our interpretations and personality. How can there be a right or wrong way to follow Jesus when God puts in our hearts and minds what's right for each of us. Faith can be expressed in different ways, and each approach can be valid and meaningful.

12. Parable of the Two Sons – Mathew 21 28-32

But what think ye? A certain man had two sons; and he came to the first, and said, Son, go work to day in my vineyard.

²⁹ He answered and said, I will not: but afterward he repented, and went.³⁰ And he came to the second, and said likewise. And he answered and said, I go, sir: and went not.

³¹ Whether of them twain did the will of his father? They say unto him, The first. Jesus saith unto them, Verily I say unto you, That the publicans and the harlots go into the kingdom of God before you.³² For John came unto you in the way of righteousness, and ye believed him not: but the publicans and the harlots believed him: and ye, when ye had seen it, repented not afterward, that ye might believe him.

SUMMARY

The Parable of the Two Sons is a story Jesus told about a father who asked his two sons to work in the family vineyard. The first son said he wouldn't do it, but later changed his mind and went to work. The second son said he would go, but he didn't actually go and work. Jesus then asked which of the two sons did what the father wanted.

INTERPRETATION

The traditional meaning of this parable is that our actions are more important than our words. It's not enough to just say we will do something good; we must actually do it. This story teaches us to be honest and responsible, and to follow through on our promises, just like the first son who ended up working in the vineyard.

An additional insight is that it teaches us about the importance of second chances and forgiveness. The first son initially refused to work, but he realized his mistake and made things right by actually doing the work. This story reminds us that people can change and that we should be willing to give them a chance to prove themselves, just like the father in the story gave his first son a chance to make up for his earlier refusal.

PERSONAL THOUGHTS

The Parable of the Two Sons illustrates a simple but profound truth: our actions speak louder than our words. A great movie that illustrates this is "Forrest Gump." In the film, the title character, played by Tom Hanks, is far from eloquent in speech, but his actions throughout his life demonstrate kindness, loyalty, bravery, and integrity. Despite his simple words, Forrest's deeds have a profound impact on the lives of those around him. In our family, we have a son on the autism spectrum. As a young man, he noticed that people's words were not always reliable and that they didn't always follow through. When it was Debbie or me, he didn't hesitate to call us out on it. This helped us realize we didn't always follow through and encouraged us to work harder at keeping our commitments. This parable reminds us that what we do matters more than what we say, and it challenges us to ensure our actions align with our words.

13. Parable of the New Cloth on an Old Garment – Mark 2 21

No man also seweth a piece of new cloth on an old garment: else the new piece that filled it up taketh away from the old, and the rent is made worse.

Summary

The Parable of the New Cloth on an Old Garment is a short story Jesus told about putting a new piece of cloth on an old garment. When you do that, the new cloth will shrink when it's washed, and it will tear away from the old garment, making the hole even bigger.

Interpretation

The traditional meaning of this parable is that new teachings often require a new perspective rather than being constrained by old traditions. Jesus was emphasizing that his message of love and forgiveness could not be effectively embraced within a rigid interpretation of the older religious rules and practices. This was foretold by the Prophet Jeremiah in the Old Testament.

An additional insight is that it teaches us about change and being open to new ideas. Sometimes, when we try to hold onto old beliefs or ways of doing things, it can cause problems or make things worse, like the new cloth on the old garment. This story reminds us to be flexible and open to new ideas, especially when they can help us grow and become better people.

Personal Thoughts

In the early 1600s, Galileo, a renowned scientist, faced opposition from the Catholic Church for supporting the theory that the Earth revolves around the Sun. Despite his contributions to science, Galileo was accused of heresy (contradicting the established beliefs of the Catholic Church) and subjected to a trial by the Church. He was found guilty and spent the remainder of his life under house arrest, where he continued his scientific work until his death.

Today, science is progressing very quickly, and often it is challenging to understand, much as it was for people in the 1600s. While individuals may have different beliefs and perspectives, my personal belief is it's worthwhile to recognize science and the importance of evidence-based reasoning. Many good Christians choose to incorporate scientific principles into their belief system, recognizing the valuable historic contributions of scientists to our lives and our knowledge of the world. This parable reminds us that new insights and understandings can sometimes clash with established beliefs, but they can also lead to personal growth, deeper comprehension of the world around us, as well as how to become better people.

14. Parable of The Faithful Servant and the Evil Servant – Luke 12 42-48

And the Lord said, Who then is that faithful and wise steward, whom his lord shall make ruler over his household, to give them their portion of meat in due season?

[43] Blessed is that servant, whom his lord when he cometh shall find so doing.[44] Of a truth I say unto you, that he will make him ruler over all that he hath.

[45] But and if that servant say in his heart, My lord delayeth his coming; and shall begin to beat the menservants and maidens, and to eat and drink, and to be drunken;[46] The lord of that servant will come in a day when he looketh not for him, and at an hour when he is not aware, and will cut him in sunder, and will appoint him his portion with the unbelievers.

[47] And that servant, which knew his lord's will, and prepared not himself, neither did according to his will, shall be beaten with many stripes.[48] But he that knew not, and did commit things worthy of stripes, shall be beaten with few stripes. For unto whomsoever much is given, of him shall be much required: and to whom men have committed much, of him they will ask the more.

Summary

The Parable of the Faithful Servant and the Evil Servant is a story Jesus told about two different servants. The faithful servant was put in charge of his master's household and took good care of everything while the master was away. The evil servant, however, thought his master wouldn't come back soon and started to mistreat the other servants and waste his master's resources. When the master returned unexpectedly, he was pleased with the faithful servant and rewarded him, but he punished the evil servant.

Interpretation

The traditional meaning of this parable is that we should always be responsible and do our best to serve God, even when it seems like Jesus' return is far away. We should treat others kindly and use the resources and opportunities we have to do good.

An additional insight is that it teaches us about the consequences of our actions. The faithful servant was rewarded for his good behavior, while the evil servant faced punishment for his poor choices. This story reminds us that our actions have consequences, and it's important to make good choices and be responsible in our daily lives to enjoy the rewards and blessings that come from living a life that follows Jesus' example.

Personal Thoughts

In my work life, I found that even if I didn't like my boss, it was beneficial to be a good employee and work hard. Often, that boss was soon replaced by a better one, and I was thankful that my hard work resulted in good reviews and a solid reputation. Additionally, there is self-satisfaction and happiness in a job well done. Moreover, if at some point you want to move on to new employment, the reputation you've built by being responsible and working hard will provide better opportunities. This parable teaches the value of diligence and integrity in all situations, regardless of the circumstances.

15. Parable of the Talents – Mathew 25 14-30 (also known as Parable of the Minas)

For the kingdom of heaven is as a man travelling into a far country, who called his own servants, and delivered unto them his goods.

[15] And unto one he gave five talents, to another two, and to another one; to every man according to his several ability; and straightway took his journey. [16] Then he that had received the five talents went and traded with the same, and made them other five talents.

[17] And likewise he that had received two, he also gained other two. [18] But he that had received one went and digged in the earth, and hid his lord's money.

[19] After a long time the lord of those servants cometh, and reckoneth with them. [20] And so he that had received five talents came and brought other five talents, saying, Lord, thou deliveredst unto me five talents: behold, I have gained beside them five talents more.

[21] His lord said unto him, Well done, thou good and faithful servant: thou hast been faithful over a few things, I will make thee ruler over many things: enter thou into the joy of thy lord. [22] He also that had received two talents came and said, Lord, thou deliveredst unto me two talents: behold, I have gained two other talents beside them.

[23] His lord said unto him, Well done, good and faithful servant; thou hast been faithful over a few things, I will make thee ruler over many things: enter thou into the joy of thy lord. [24] Then he which had received the one talent came and said, Lord, I knew thee that thou art an hard man, reaping where thou hast not sown, and gathering where thou hast not strawed:

[25] And I was afraid, and went and hid thy talent in the earth: lo, there thou hast that is thine. [26] His lord answered and said unto him, Thou wicked and slothful servant, thou knewest that I reap where I sowed not, and gather where I have not strawed:

[27] Thou oughtest therefore to have put my money to the exchangers, and then at my coming I should have received mine own with usury. [28] Take therefore the talent from him, and give it unto him which hath ten talents.

[29] For unto every one that hath shall be given, and he shall have abundance: but from him that hath not shall be taken away even that which he hath. [30] And cast ye the unprofitable servant into outer darkness: there shall be weeping and gnashing of teeth.

SUMMARY

The Parable of the Talents is a story Jesus told about a man who was going on a trip. Before he left, he gave three of his servants different amounts of money, called "talents", to take care of while he was gone. The first two servants used the money to make more money, but the third servant just hid his talents in the ground. When the man returned, he was happy with the first two servants and rewarded them, but he was angry with the third servant for not using the money wisely.

INTERPRETATION

The traditional meaning of this parable is we should use the gifts and abilities God has given us to do good things and help others. Just like the first two servants used their money wisely, we should also use our God given skills and abilities to make a positive impact in the world and show our love for God.

An additional insight is that it teaches us about the importance of taking risks and not being afraid to try new things. The first two servants took a chance and used their money to make more money, while the third servant was too scared to do anything with his. This story encourages us to be brave, to step out of our comfort zones, and to make the most of the opportunities that come our way, so that we can grow and become better people.

PERSONAL THOUGHTS

Debbie has a saying she often reiterates in times of big life decisions: "When we're old and sitting in our rockers, will we be glad we tried or wish we had?" Regardless of success or failure, years later we've always been glad we tried. The first two servants, who invest and grow their talents, exemplify the benefits of hard work, creativity, and risk-taking. Their efforts lead to success in the eyes of the man they served and in aspects of their own life. Conversely, the third servant represents those who, due to fear or apathy, fail to utilize their potential. His inaction and resulting stagnation serve as a caution against letting fear or laziness hinder our growth and achievements.

16. Parable of the Sheep and Goats – Mathew 25 31-36

When the Son of man shall come in his glory, and all the holy angels with him, then shall he sit upon the throne of his glory:

32 And before him shall be gathered all nations: and he shall separate them one from another, as a shepherd divideth his sheep from the goats:

33 And he shall set the sheep on his right hand, but the goats on the left.34 Then shall the King say unto them on his right hand, Come, ye blessed of my Father, inherit the kingdom prepared for you from the foundation of the world:

35 For I was an hungred, and ye gave me meat: I was thirsty, and ye gave me drink: I was a stranger, and ye took me in:36 Naked, and ye clothed me: I was sick, and ye visited me: I was in prison, and ye came unto me.

37 Then shall the righteous answer him, saying, Lord, when saw we thee an hungred, and fed thee? or thirsty, and gave thee drink?38 When saw we thee a stranger, and took thee in? or naked, and clothed thee?

39 Or when saw we thee sick, or in prison, and came unto thee?40 And the King shall answer and say unto them, Verily I say unto you, Inasmuch as ye have done it unto one of the least of these my brethren, ye have done it unto me.

41 Then shall he say also unto them on the left hand, Depart from me, ye cursed, into everlasting fire, prepared for the devil and his angels:42 For I was an hungred, and ye gave me no meat: I was thirsty, and ye gave me no drink:

43 I was a stranger, and ye took me not in: naked, and ye clothed me not: sick, and in prison, and ye visited me not.44 Then shall they also answer him, saying, Lord, when saw we thee an hungred, or athirst, or a stranger, or naked, or sick, or in prison, and did not minister unto thee?

45 Then shall he answer them, saying, Verily I say unto you, Inasmuch as ye did it not to one of the least of these, ye did it not to me.46 And these shall go away into everlasting punishment: but the righteous into life eternal.

Summary

In the Parable of the Sheep and the Goats Jesus describes the final judgment. He will separate people as a shepherd separates the sheep from the goats. The sheep, representing good people, will be placed on His right and will inherit the Kingdom prepared for them. They are commended for acts of kindness and mercy: feeding the hungry, giving drink to the thirsty, welcoming strangers, clothing the naked, caring for the sick, and visiting those in prison. Conversely, the goats, representing the unrighteous, will be placed on His left and will be sent away into eternal punishment for failing to do these acts of compassion.

Interpretation

The traditional meaning of this parable is to show the importance of compassionate actions as expressions of genuine faith. It teaches that the true followers of Christ will be recognized by their deeds of mercy and kindness towards others, especially those in need.

An additional insight focuses on God's love of all people. This suggests that the parable is not just about individual acts of kindness but also about recognizing Christ in all people, especially the marginalized and oppressed, and people who may have alternative beliefs than you. It challenges believers to see every human being as being created by God and deserving of dignity and compassion.

Personal Thoughts

When I was young, my dad and I took some food to some poor people on Christmas. At one of the houses, which was extremely run down in a very poor area, an old man answered the door. He was on oxygen, his house was in terrible shape, as was his furniture. But he had a modern large screen color TV. I told my dad I didn't see why he was spending his money on an expensive color TV when he had so many other needs for his money. My dad looked at me and said, "He has almost nothing; let him have something nice he can enjoy." I learned a lot from that. My dad's lesson taught me to think beyond what might initially appear obvious and to imagine yourself in the shoes of others, thus better understanding their actions and deeper needs.

17. Parable of the Growing Seed – Mark 4 26-29

And he said, So is the kingdom of God, as if a man should cast seed into the ground;

²⁷ And should sleep, and rise night and day, and the seed should spring and grow up, he knoweth not how.

²⁸ For the earth bringeth forth fruit of herself; first the blade, then the ear, after that the full corn in the ear.

²⁹ But when the fruit is brought forth, immediately he putteth in the sickle, because the harvest is come.

SUMMARY

The Parable of the Growing Seed is a story Jesus told about a farmer who plants seeds in his field. The seeds start to grow, first into small plants, then bigger plants, and finally into grain. The farmer doesn't know exactly how the plants grow, but when they are ready, he harvests the grain.

INTERPRETATION

The traditional meaning of this parable is that God's kingdom grows gradually and mysteriously, just like the seeds in the farmer's field. We may not always understand how it grows or when it will be fully grown, but God is always working to help it grow.

An additional insight is that it teaches us about patience and trust. Just like the farmer waits for the seeds to grow into plants and then into grain, we also need to be patient and trust that God is working in our lives and in the world around us. This story reminds us that growth takes time and that we should have faith in God's plan, even when we don't fully understand it.

PERSONAL THOUGHTS

Our son that is on the autism spectrum graduated from high school without many of the life skills typically expected for college or work at that age. Through the guidance of a wonderful counselor, we learned to be patient with him, to continue teaching and modeling positive life skills, and to never give up on him. Over time, he became an active learner, setting his own pace for progress. Now at 41, our son has developed many life skills we once doubted he would ever acquire, and in some areas, he is even more adept than we are!

Debbie and I feel this parable teaches the importance of patience and trust in natural growth. It reflects the reality that growth, whether in nature, education, work, or personal endeavors, takes time and isn't always consistent or visible in daily changes. This parable encourages us to be patient and to trust in the process of life, understanding that some things develop at their own pace.

18. PARABLE OF THE LAMP – MARK 4 21-25

And he said unto them, Is a candle brought to be put under a bushel, or under a bed? and not to be set on a candlestick?

²² For there is nothing hid, which shall not be manifested; neither was any thing kept secret, but that it should come abroad.

²³ If any man have ears to hear, let him hear.

²⁴ And he said unto them, Take heed what ye hear: with what measure ye mete, it shall be measured to you: and unto you that hear shall more be given.

²⁵ For he that hath, to him shall be given: and he that hath not, from him shall be taken even that which he hath.

SUMMARY

The Parable of the Lamp is a story Jesus told about a lamp that is meant to be put on a stand so it can give light to the whole room. No one puts the lamp under a basket or hides it because that would defeat its purpose. The Lamp's light should be visible and useful to everyone.

INTERPRETATION

The traditional meaning of this parable is that we should let our goodness and the love of God shine through us, just like the lamp on the stand gives light to the room. We should share our faith, kindness, and love with others so that they can see the good things God has done in our lives.

An additional insight is that it teaches us about the importance of being true to ourselves and living our lives with purpose. Just like the lamp is meant to provide light, we all have unique gifts and talents that we should use to make a positive impact in the world. This story encourages us to embrace our individuality and use our abilities to help others and make the world a better place.

PERSONAL THOUGHTS

Susan Boyle first stepped on the stage of *Britain's Got Talent* at age 48, having only sung in church and at local events. Being on the autism spectrum and not fitting the industry's conventional image of a rising star, she initially faced low expectations. However, on April 11, 2009, she captivated the world with her unforgettable voice, launching a music career that defied all odds. Her debut album went on to become the UK's biggest-selling first release, featuring enduring favorites such as "I Dreamed a Dream," "Amazing Grace," "Hallelujah," and "You Raise Me Up".

Like a lamp that brings light to a room, we shouldn't hesitate to make efforts to share our skills or knowledge which might be beneficial to others. Susan Boyle's story reminds us that even when we face obstacles, our unique talents can shine brightly and make a significant impact.

19. PARABLE OF THE GOOD SAMARITAN – LUKE 10 29-37

But he, willing to justify himself, said unto Jesus, And who is my neighbour?

³⁰ And Jesus answering said, A certain man went down from Jerusalem to Jericho, and fell among thieves, which stripped him of his raiment, and wounded him, and departed, leaving him half dead.

³¹ And by chance there came down a certain priest that way: and when he saw him, he passed by on the other side.³² And likewise a Levite, when he was at the place, came and looked on him, and passed by on the other side.

³³ But a certain Samaritan, as he journeyed, came where he was: and when he saw him, he had compassion on him,³⁴ And went to him, and bound up his wounds, pouring in oil and wine, and set him on his own beast, and brought him to an inn, and took care of him.

³⁵ And on the morrow when he departed, he took out two pence, and gave them to the host, and said unto him, Take care of him; and whatsoever thou spendest more, when I come again, I will repay thee.³⁶ Which now of these three, thinkest thou, was neighbour unto him that fell among the thieves?

³⁷ And he said, He that shewed mercy on him. Then said Jesus unto him, Go, and do thou likewise.

Summary

The Parable of the Good Samaritan is a story Jesus told about a man who was traveling and got attacked by robbers. They beat him up and left him hurt on the side of the road. A priest and a Levite passed by, but they didn't help the man. Then a Samaritan came along, and even though Samaritans and the injured man's people didn't usually get along, the Samaritan stopped to help the hurt man. He took care of him, brought him to an inn, and paid for his stay.

Interpretation

The traditional meaning of this parable is that we should be kind and help others, no matter who they are or where they come from. Jesus taught that everyone is our neighbor, and we should show love and compassion to all people, just like the Good Samaritan did.

An additional insight is that it teaches us about the importance of putting our beliefs into action. The priest and the Levite, who were religious leaders, didn't help the injured man. But the Samaritan, who might not have been expected to help, showed kindness and love through his actions. This story reminds us that it's not just what we say or think that matters, but our actions, how we treat others and what we do to make a difference in their lives.

Personal Thoughts

In today's world, there can be a fear of stopping to help or a belief that someone else will step in. Visiting my son in Los Angeles some years ago, we came to a busy intersection where a homeless man had fallen and couldn't get up. A pedestrian had stopped and was blocking traffic to prevent the man from being run over, and a police car was pulling up. My son, who had been a paramedic in earlier years, pulled over and ran to check if further help was needed. It turned out the man was having a seizure, and my son was able to assist and stay with him. Initially, the police wanted to move the man off the street, but my son insisted they wait until he had recovered. This situation involved many good Samaritans, but I was particularly proud of my son for stopping even when help seemed to be on the way. His assistance was crucial and made a real difference.

20. Parable of the Friend at Midnight – Luke 11 5-8

And he said unto them, Which of you shall have a friend, and shall go unto him at midnight, and say unto him, Friend, lend me three loaves;

⁶ For a friend of mine in his journey is come to me, and I have nothing to set before him?

⁷ And he from within shall answer and say, Trouble me not: the door is now shut, and my children are with me in bed; I cannot rise and give thee.

⁸ I say unto you, Though he will not rise and give him, because he is his friend, yet because of his importunity he will rise and give him as many as he needeth.

SUMMARY

The Parable of the Friend at Midnight is a story Jesus told about a man who went to his friend's house late at night to ask for some bread because he had a visitor and nothing to feed him. The friend, who was already in bed with his family, didn't want to get up at first, but because the man kept asking, he finally got up and gave him the bread.

INTERPRETATION

The traditional meaning of this parable is that we should be persistent in our prayers and keep asking God for what we need. Just like the man who kept asking his friend for bread, we should keep praying and trusting that God will answer our prayers.

An additional insight is that it teaches us about the importance of friendship and helping others in need. The friend, even though he was in bed and didn't want to get up, eventually helped his friend because he cared about him. This story reminds us that we should be there for our friends and help them when they need us, even if it's not convenient or easy for us at the time.

PERSONAL THOUGHTS

We've all experienced situations where our requests for help seem to be ignored or met with frustration. For instance, trying to get assistance from the cable or phone company, securing a timely doctor's appointment, or finding a plumber or electrician who can come promptly. In these situations, it's essential to remember that the people we are asking for help are just like us. They might be overwhelmed by their workload, dealing with personal issues, or facing other challenges that affect their ability to respond sympathetically or promptly. The key is to be persistent in a kind and friendly manner, regardless of their initial response. We don't know their circumstances, but maintaining a steady and compassionate approach can lead to a positive outcome. Our persistence, coupled with understanding and patience, can often yield better results than anger or frustration ever could.

21. Parable of the Weeds – Mathew 13 24-30

Another parable put he forth unto them, saying, The kingdom of heaven is likened unto a man which sowed good seed in his field:

[25] But while men slept, his enemy came and sowed tares among the wheat, and went his way.[26] But when the blade was sprung up, and brought forth fruit, then appeared the tares also.

[27] So the servants of the householder came and said unto him, Sir, didst not thou sow good seed in thy field? from whence then hath it tares?[28] He said unto them, An enemy hath done this. The servants said unto him, Wilt thou then that we go and gather them up?

[29] But he said, Nay; lest while ye gather up the tares, ye root up also the wheat with them.[30] Let both grow together until the harvest: and in the time of harvest I will say to the reapers, Gather ye together first the tares, and bind them in bundles to burn them: but gather the wheat into my barn.

SUMMARY

The Parable of the Weeds is a story Jesus told about a farmer who planted good seeds in his field. But while he was sleeping, an enemy came and planted weeds among the wheat. When the plants began to grow, the farmer's workers saw the weeds and asked if they should pull them out. The farmer said no, because they might also pull out the good wheat. He told them to let both grow until the harvest when they would separate the weeds from the wheat.

INTERPRETATION

The traditional meaning of this parable is that in the world, there are both good people (like the wheat) and bad people (like the weeds). God allows them to live together, but at the end of time, there will be a judgment, and the good people will be separated from the bad. The good people will be rewarded, and the bad people will be punished.

An additional insight is that it teaches us to be patient and trust God's plan. We shouldn't try to judge others or take matters into our own hands. Instead, we should focus on becoming good and faithful individuals and leave the judgment to God when the time comes. This way, we can learn to live together with others, despite their imperfections and ours, and trust that God will ultimately bring justice and peace.

PERSONAL THOUGHTS

To me, this parable teaches patience and understanding. We often don't know the full story behind someone's actions, so it's wise not to rush to judgment. For example, sometimes we receive an email or text that feels upsetting. A good rule of thumb is to wait until the next morning before responding. Often, when we reread it, we realize there was no ill intent. Also, even if it still bothers us, waiting helps us respond calmly and respectfully, in a way that we can be proud of and that aligns with what Jesus might expect from us.

22. PARABLE OF THE UNFORGIVING SERVANT – MATHEW 18 23-35

Therefore is the kingdom of heaven likened unto a certain king, which would take account of his servants.

[24] And when he had begun to reckon, one was brought unto him, which owed him ten thousand talents.[25] But forasmuch as he had not to pay, his lord commanded him to be sold, and his wife, and children, and all that he had, and payment to be made.

[26] The servant therefore fell down, and worshipped him, saying, Lord, have patience with me, and I will pay thee all.[27] Then the lord of that servant was moved with compassion, and loosed him, and forgave him the debt.

[28] But the same servant went out, and found one of his fellowservants, which owed him an hundred pence: and he laid hands on him, and took him by the throat, saying, Pay me that thou owest.[29] And his fellowservant fell down at his feet, and besought him, saying, Have patience with me, and I will pay thee all.

[30] And he would not: but went and cast him into prison, till he should pay the debt.[31] So when his fellowservants saw what was done, they were very sorry, and came and told unto their lord all that was done.

[32] Then his lord, after that he had called him, said unto him, O thou wicked servant, I forgave thee all that debt, because thou desiredst me:[33] Shouldest not thou also have had compassion on thy fellowservant, even as I had pity on thee?

[34] And his lord was wroth, and delivered him to the tormentors, till he should pay all that was due unto him.[35] So likewise shall my heavenly Father do also unto you, if ye from your hearts forgive not every one his brother their trespasses.

SUMMARY

The Parable of the Unforgiving Servant is a story Jesus told about a servant who owed a lot of money to his king. The servant couldn't pay it back, so the king was going to sell him and his family as slaves. The servant begged for mercy, and the king forgave his debt. But then, the servant went and found another servant who owed him a small amount of money. Instead of forgiving the debt like the king did for him, he had the other servant thrown in jail until the debt was paid. When the king found out, he was very angry and punished the unforgiving servant.

INTERPRETATION

The traditional meaning of this parable is that we should be willing to forgive others, just like God forgives us. When we make mistakes and ask for forgiveness, God is kind and merciful. In the same way, we should also be kind and forgiving to the people around us, even if they make mistakes or hurt us.

An additional insight of this parable is that it teaches us about the importance of showing compassion and understanding to others. The unforgiving servant didn't treat the other servant with kindness or forgiveness, even though he himself had been forgiven. This story reminds us to treat others with the same kindness and mercy that we hope to receive, and not to hold grudges or be harsh when others make mistakes.

PERSONAL THOUGHTS

Reflecting on the Parable of the Unforgiving Servant, I'm reminded of the importance of reciprocating the kindness and forgiveness we receive. We've all been in situations where we've been grateful for being helped by others or forgiven for our mistakes. This parable underscores the significance of passing on that forgiveness to others. By doing so, we can create a ripple effect of generosity and kindness, encouraging others to "pay it forward" as well. Such actions not only uplift those around us but also foster a more compassionate and understanding community.

23. Parable of the Ten Virgins
Mathew 25 1-13

Then shall the kingdom of heaven be likened unto ten virgins, which took their lamps, and went forth to meet the bridegroom.

2 And five of them were wise, and five were foolish.

3 They that were foolish took their lamps, and took no oil with them:4 But the wise took oil in their vessels with their lamps.

5 While the bridegroom tarried, they all slumbered and slept.6 And at midnight there was a cry made, Behold, the bridegroom cometh; go ye out to meet him.

7 Then all those virgins arose, and trimmed their lamps.8 And the foolish said unto the wise, Give us of your oil; for our lamps are gone out.

9 But the wise answered, saying, Not so; lest there be not enough for us and you: but go ye rather to them that sell, and buy for yourselves.10 And while they went to buy, the bridegroom came; and they that were ready went in with him to the marriage: and the door was shut.

11 Afterward came also the other virgins, saying, Lord, Lord, open to us.12 But he answered and said, Verily I say unto you, I know you not.

13 Watch therefore, for ye know neither the day nor the hour wherein the Son of man cometh.

SUMMARY

The Parable of the Ten Virgins is a story Jesus told about ten young women who were waiting for a bridegroom to arrive at a wedding. They all had lamps to light his way, but only five of them brought extra oil for their lamps. The bridegroom took longer than expected, and while they were waiting, they all fell asleep. When the bridegroom arrived, the five wise women who had extra oil could light their lamps, but the five foolish women didn't have enough oil and had to go buy more. While they were gone, the bridegroom came and the wise women went into the wedding feast, but the foolish women were locked out when they returned.

INTERPRETATION

The traditional meaning of this parable is that we should always be prepared for Jesus' return, just like the wise young women were prepared with extra oil for their lamps. We don't know when He will come, so it's important to be ready by following His teachings and living good lives.

An additional insight is that it teaches us about the importance of being responsible and making good choices. The wise women in the story thought ahead and made sure they were prepared, while the foolish women did not plan and ended up missing the wedding feast. This story reminds us that we need to take responsibility for our actions and make wise decisions to fully experience the blessings and opportunities that God has in store for us.

PERSONAL THOUGHTS

Since the founding of the Boy Scouts, their motto has been "Be Prepared." We all know the importance of being prepared and planning ahead, as illustrated in this Parable. The challenge lies not in knowing this, but in doing it! An example in our family is our hurricane kit. We live in a hurricane zone and have a tendency to raid our supplies during the year but then forget to replace what we removed. From now on, whenever I read this parable, I'm hopeful it will remind me to check and restock my hurricane kit in addition to the lesson of being prepared for Jesus and many other possible life events.

24. Parable of The Great Banquet – Luke 14 15-24

And when one of them that sat at meat with him heard these things, he said unto him, Blessed is he that shall eat bread in the kingdom of God.

[16] Then said he unto him, A certain man made a great supper, and bade many:

[17] And sent his servant at supper time to say to them that were bidden, Come; for all things are now ready.[18] And they all with one consent began to make excuse. The first said unto him, I have bought a piece of ground, and I must needs go and see it: I pray thee have me excused.

[19] And another said, I have bought five yoke of oxen, and I go to prove them: I pray thee have me excused.[20] And another said, I have married a wife, and therefore I cannot come.

[21] So that servant came, and shewed his lord these things. Then the master of the house being angry said to his servant, Go out quickly into the streets and lanes of the city, and bring in hither the poor, and the maimed, and the halt, and the blind.[22] And the servant said, Lord, it is done as thou hast commanded, and yet there is room.

[23] And the lord said unto the servant, Go out into the highways and hedges, and compel them to come in, that my house may be filled.[24] For I say unto you, That none of those men which were bidden shall taste of my supper.

SUMMARY

The Parable of the Great Banquet is a story Jesus told about a man who planned a big party and invited lots of guests. But when the time came for the party, the guests started making excuses for why they couldn't come. So, the man told his servant to go out and invite the poor, the disabled, and others who were usually left out. They came to the party and enjoyed the feast, while the original guests missed out.

INTERPRETATION

The traditional meaning of this parable is that God invites everyone to be a part of His kingdom, but some people choose not to accept the invitation because they are too busy with their own lives or think they are too important. The people who are humble and recognize their need for God are the ones who will enjoy the great banquet in God's kingdom.

An additional insight is that it teaches us about the importance of being open and welcoming to everyone, regardless of their background or social status. The man in the story wanted his banquet to be full, so he invited people who were usually left out of such events. This story reminds us to treat everyone with kindness and respect, and to share God's love and blessings with all people, not just those who seem important or worthy in the eyes of the world.

PERSONAL THOUGHTS

If you are particularly smart, talented, successful, or athletic, it is easy to subconsciously consider yourself part of a higher class of people, thinking you are better than others. This parable serves as a reminder that those in your immediate circle may not always be the best or most reliable people around you. It's important to socialize and interact with all types of people to keep yourself grounded. By doing so, you may find it easier to be empathetic and a good Christian. This parable encourages us to embrace humility and inclusiveness, recognizing the value in everyone, regardless of their status.

25. Parable of The Cost of Discipleship – Luke 14 28-33

For which of you, intending to build a tower, sitteth not down first, and counteth the cost, whether he have sufficient to finish it?

29 Lest haply, after he hath laid the foundation, and is not able to finish it, all that behold it begin to mock him,30 Saying, This man began to build, and was not able to finish.

31 Or what king, going to make war against another king, sitteth not down first, and consulteth whether he be able with ten thousand to meet him that cometh against him with twenty thousand?32 Or else, while the other is yet a great way off, he sendeth an ambassage, and desireth conditions of peace.

33 So likewise, whosoever he be of you that forsaketh not all that he hath, he cannot be my disciple.

SUMMARY

The Parable of the Cost of Discipleship isn't a story like other parables, but rather Jesus is teaching about what it means to follow Him. Jesus explained that being His disciple is a big commitment and requires putting Him first, even before family and personal desires. He used the examples of a person building a tower or a king going to war, saying that they should count the cost before starting so they can finish what they began.

INTERPRETATION

The traditional meaning of this teaching is that following Jesus isn't always easy, and we should be prepared to make sacrifices and put Him first in our lives. We need to consider if we're truly willing to commit ourselves to living as His disciples, knowing that it might be challenging at times.

An additional insight is that it reminds us of the importance of being dedicated and committed to our faith. Just like the person building the tower or the king going to war, we need to be fully prepared and committed to our spiritual journey. This means focusing on our relationship with God, growing in our faith, and sharing His love with others, even when it's difficult or requires personal sacrifices.

PERSONAL THOUGHTS

Every activity we engage in comes with a cost that we need to be aware of. When I was 41, with a wife and two boys, I was promoted to a position that was a big step up for me. However, I quickly learned that there was a downside: I was on call 24/7 and working countless hours. Every new activity we take on must displace something else in our lives. A new job might pay more money, but will it require more time, taking away from our family? A new hobby might be beneficial for one aspect of our mental well-being, but what is it replacing in terms of time with our spouse or kids, and is it worth it? A new sports car might be fun and prestigious, but will we have to cut back on our charitable contributions to afford it? This parable reminds me to consider what might be sacrificed for what appears to be a big jump forward in life. It's a call to carefully evaluate our decisions and ensure we are prioritizing what truly matters.

26. Parable of The Lost Coin – Luke 15 8-10

Either what woman having ten pieces of silver, if she lose one piece, doth not light a candle, and sweep the house, and seek diligently till she find it?

9 And when she hath found it, she calleth her friends and her neighbours together, saying, Rejoice with me; for I have found the piece which I had lost.

10 Likewise, I say unto you, there is joy in the presence of the angels of God over one sinner that repenteth.

SUMMARY

The Parable of the Lost Coin is a story Jesus told about a woman who had ten coins and lost one of them. She lit a lamp, swept the house, and searched carefully until she finally found the lost coin. She was so happy that she called her friends and neighbors to celebrate with her.

INTERPRETATION

The traditional meaning of this parable is that God cares about each and every one of us, even when we feel lost or far away from Him. Just like the woman who searched for her lost coin, God searches for us and rejoices when we are found and come back to Him.

An additional insight is that it teaches us about the value of persistence and never giving up. The woman didn't stop looking for her lost coin until she found it, showing her determination and commitment. This story reminds us to keep searching and working towards our goals, whether they are spiritual, personal, or related to helping others, and to celebrate our successes along the way.

PERSONAL THOUGHTS

I had a very good friend for about 20 years, but then we moved apart, and I lost track of him. I didn't make much effort to stay in touch and had no idea where he was for a few years. One day, his daughter contacted us to say he had cancer and gave us his address. When I visited, he was already close to death. I was able to talk with him and be with him for a couple of days before he passed away. I wish I had tried to locate him earlier and stay in touch. A lost friend is far more valuable than a lost coin.

27. PARABLE OF THE PRODIGAL SON – LUKE 15 11-32

And he said, A certain man had two sons:

¹² And the younger of them said to his father, Father, give me the portion of goods that falleth to me. And he divided unto them his living. ¹³ And not many days after the younger son gathered all together, and took his journey into a far country, and there wasted his substance with riotous living.

¹⁴ And when he had spent all, there arose a mighty famine in that land; and he began to be in want. ¹⁵ And he went and joined himself to a citizen of that country; and he sent him into his fields to feed swine. ¹⁶ And he would fain have filled his belly with the husks that the swine did eat: and no man gave unto him. ¹⁷ And when he came to himself, he said, How many hired servants of my father's have bread enough and to spare, and I perish with hunger!

¹⁸ I will arise and go to my father, and will say unto him, Father, I have sinned against heaven, and before thee, ¹⁹ And am no more worthy to be called thy son: make me as one of thy hired servants. ²⁰ And he arose, and came to his father. But when he was yet a great way off, his father saw him, and had compassion, and ran, and fell on his neck, and kissed him.

²¹ And the son said unto him, Father, I have sinned against heaven, and in thy sight, and am no more worthy to be called thy son. ²² But the father said to his servants, Bring forth the best robe, and put it on him; and put a ring on his hand, and shoes on his feet: ²³ And bring hither the fatted calf, and kill it; and let us eat, and be merry:

²⁴ For this my son was dead, and is alive again; he was lost, and is found. And they began to be merry. ²⁵ Now his elder son was in the field: and as he came and drew nigh to the house, he heard musick and dancing. ²⁶ And he called one of the servants, and asked what these things meant.

²⁷ And he said unto him, Thy brother is come; and thy father hath killed the fatted calf, because he hath received him safe and sound. ²⁸ And he was angry, and would not go in: therefore came his father out, and intreated him. ²⁹ And he answering said to his father, Lo, these many years do I serve thee, neither transgressed I at any time thy commandment: and yet thou never gavest me a kid, that I might make merry with my friends:

³⁰ But as soon as this thy son was come, which hath devoured thy living with harlots, thou hast killed for him the fatted calf. ³¹ And he said unto him, Son, thou art ever with me, and all that I have is thine. ³² It was meet that we should make merry, and be glad: for this thy brother was dead, and is alive again; and was lost, and is found.

SUMMARY

The Parable of the Prodigal Son is a story Jesus told about a man and his two sons. The younger son asked his father for his share of the family's money and left home to live on his own. He spent all his money on wild parties and fancy things. Eventually, he ran out of money. He realized he made a big mistake and decided to go back home and apologize to his father. To his surprise, his father welcomed him back with open arms and threw a big party for him. The Elder son, who had stayed home and been good and served his father well became angry and jealous. He felt he had been a good son while his younger brother had not, yet his father welcomed the younger son home and threw a big party.

INTERPRETATION

The traditional meaning of this parable is that God loves us and is always ready to forgive us when we make mistakes if we are truly sorry and want to change. Just like the father in the story welcomed his son back, God welcomes us back when we turn to Him.

An additional insight is that it teaches us about the importance of giving forgiveness and second chances for people in our lives. The father in the story didn't hold a grudge against his younger son for his mistakes but forgave him and celebrated his return. Also we see the father has enough love for both sons.

PERSONAL THOUGHTS

Debbie has always had a philosophy to never judge people or let their past actions dictate how she treats them in the future. As a teenager and young woman, a relative of Debbie's got into trouble, treated others disrespectfully, was not dependable, and became disliked and alienated by some family members. Regardless, Debbie always treated her with the same respect and love, guided by this parable. If she needed help or a small loan, Debbie was there for her. Over the years, this young woman matured, found faith, worked her way through college, and became a wonderful woman and mother. She is now a welcomed member of the entire family, thanks in part to Debbie's unconditional love. This parable teaches us the importance of forgiveness and unconditional support, and the transformative power they can have on people's lives.

28. Parable of the Dishonest Manager – Luke 16 1-13

And he said also unto his disciples, There was a certain rich man, which had a steward; and the same was accused unto him that he had wasted his goods.[2] And he called him, and said unto him, How is it that I hear this of thee? give an account of thy stewardship; for thou mayest be no longer steward.[3] Then the steward said within himself, What shall I do? for my lord taketh away from me the stewardship: I cannot dig; to beg I am ashamed.

[4] I am resolved what to do, that, when I am put out of the stewardship, they may receive me into their houses.[5] So he called every one of his lord›s debtors unto him, and said unto the first, How much owest thou unto my lord?[6] And he said, An hundred measures of oil. And he said unto him, Take thy bill, and sit down quickly, and write fifty.

[7] Then said he to another, And how much owest thou? And he said, An hundred measures of wheat. And he said unto him, Take thy bill, and write fourscore.[8] And the lord commended the unjust steward, because he had done wisely: for the children of this world are in their generation wiser than the children of light.[9] And I say unto you, Make to yourselves friends of the mammon of unrighteousness; that, when ye fail, they may receive you into everlasting habitations.

[10] He that is faithful in that which is least is faithful also in much: and he that is unjust in the least is unjust also in much.[11] If therefore ye have not been faithful in the unrighteous mammon, who will commit to your trust the true riches?[12] And if ye have not been faithful in that which is another man›s, who shall give you that which is your own?

[13] No servant can serve two masters: for either he will hate the one, and love the other; or else he will hold to the one, and despise the other. Ye cannot serve God and mammon.

Summary

The Parable of the Dishonest Manager is a story Jesus told about a manager who was about to lose his job because he was wasting his boss's money. Knowing he'd be out of work soon; he came up with a clever plan. He went to the people who owed his boss money and reduced their debts, making them like him and owe him favors. When his boss found out, he was actually impressed by the manager's cleverness.

Interpretation

The traditional meaning of this parable is that we should use our resources and abilities wisely to plan for our future. Jesus wants us to be smart and think ahead, like the dishonest manager, but of course, without being dishonest or doing anything wrong.

An additional insight is that it teaches us to make the most of the opportunities we have, even in difficult situations. The manager in the story used his position and connections to secure a better future for himself, despite his mistakes. The confusing part of this parable is it seems to praise dishonesty, but that's not the point Jesus is making. The main point Jesus is making to his followers is to use their resources, time, and abilities now to make a positive impact and prepare for their eternal future. The dishonest manager is used as an example of resourcefulness, not as a model of ethical behavior.

Personal Thoughts

Reflecting on this parable, I'm reminded of moments in my own life where resourcefulness and persistence were crucial in overcoming obstacles. It teaches that even when we create our own problems or contribute to our own challenges, we can still find ways to persevere and work toward positive outcomes. This interpretation deepens my appreciation for resilience and adaptability, encouraging me to approach adversity with a determined and positive mindset.

29. Parable of The Rich Man and Lazarus – Luke 16 19-26

¹⁹ There was a certain rich man, which was clothed in purple and fine linen, and fared sumptuously every day:

²⁰ And there was a certain beggar named Lazarus, which was laid at his gate, full of sores,

²¹ And desiring to be fed with the crumbs which fell from the rich man›s table: moreover the dogs came and licked his sores.

²² And it came to pass, that the beggar died, and was carried by the angels into Abraham›s bosom: the rich man also died, and was buried;

²³ And in hell he lift up his eyes, being in torments, and seeth Abraham afar off, and Lazarus in his bosom.

²⁴ And he cried and said, Father Abraham, have mercy on me, and send Lazarus, that he may dip the tip of his finger in water, and cool my tongue; for I am tormented in this flame.

²⁵ But Abraham said, Son, remember that thou in thy lifetime receivedst thy good things, and likewise Lazarus evil things: but now he is comforted, and thou art tormented.

²⁶ And beside all this, between us and you there is a great gulf fixed: so that they which would pass from hence to you cannot; neither can they pass to us, that would come from thence.

SUMMARY

The Parable of the Rich Man and Lazarus is a story Jesus told about a rich man who lived a luxurious life and a poor man named Lazarus who was sick and hungry, lying at the rich man's gate. Both men died, and Lazarus went to heaven, while the rich man ended up in a place of suffering. The rich man asked if Lazarus could come and help him, but he was told that there was a great divide between them, and nothing could be done.

INTERPRETATION

The traditional meaning of this parable is that our actions and choices on Earth have consequences in the afterlife. The rich man didn't help Lazarus when he had the chance, so he ended up suffering after death. This story teaches us to care for others and be kind while we're still alive.

An additional insight is that it reminds us not to focus only on our own comfort and wealth. The rich man lived a fancy life, but he didn't care about Lazarus, who was suffering. This story teaches us that true happiness and fulfillment come from helping others and sharing what we have, rather than just trying to make ourselves rich and comfortable.

PERSONAL THOUGHTS

We sometimes encounter beggars at street corners. We don't know why they are begging or what may have happened in their lives to lead them there. Some may be part of a scheme to take our money, some may be mentally disabled, or there could be any number of other possibilities. Rather than trying to judge and determine if they are worthy, I feel this parable guides us to help anyone in need, regardless of the circumstances as we really don't know the story of their life and how they ended up in their situation.

Our actions everyday are role modeling for our kids and everyone we encounter. We leave a small subconscious imprint on those around us that will live on even after our deaths and we've been forgotten. That's a comforting thought as we become senior citizens, knowing that our kindness and compassion continue to make a difference and live on.

30. Parable of the Persistent Widow = Luke 18 1-8

And he spake a parable unto them to this end, that men ought always to pray, and not to faint;

² Saying, There was in a city a judge, which feared not God, neither regarded man:

³ And there was a widow in that city; and she came unto him, saying, Avenge me of mine adversary. ⁴ And he would not for a while: but afterward he said within himself, Though I fear not God, nor regard man;

⁵ Yet because this widow troubleth me, I will avenge her, lest by her continual coming she weary me. ⁶ And the Lord said, Hear what the unjust judge saith.

⁷ And shall not God avenge his own elect, which cry day and night unto him, though he bear long with them? ⁸ I tell you that he will avenge them speedily. Nevertheless when the Son of man cometh, shall he find faith on the earth?

SUMMARY

The Parable of the Persistent Widow is a story Jesus told about a widow who kept going to a judge and asking him to give her justice against someone who had wronged her. The judge didn't care about her problem at first, but because she kept coming back and bothering him, he finally decided to help her just to get her to leave him alone.

INTERPRETATION

The traditional meaning of this parable is that we should never give up when we pray to God and ask Him for help. Just like the widow kept asking the judge for justice, we should keep praying and trusting that God will answer our prayers in His own time and way.

An additional insight is that it teaches us about the power of persistence and determination. The widow didn't let the judge's initial refusal stop her; she kept trying until she got what she needed. This story reminds us that we should stay strong and keep working towards our goals, even when things seem difficult, or we face obstacles along the way.

PERSONAL THOUGHTS

Thomas Edison famously said regarding his many failures prior to inventing the light bulb, "I have not failed. I've just found 10,000 ways that won't work." This mindset reflects the essence of the parable, emphasizing that persistence, even in the face of numerous setbacks, is crucial for achieving our goals and making progress in life whether it be trying to be a good husband, wife, father, student, etc. Persistence can overcome many obstacles.

31. Parable of the Pharisee and the Tax Collector – Luke 18 9-14

And he spake this parable unto certain which trusted in themselves that they were righteous, and despised others:

[10] Two men went up into the temple to pray; the one a Pharisee, and the other a publican.

[11] The Pharisee stood and prayed thus with himself, God, I thank thee, that I am not as other men are, extortioners, unjust, adulterers, or even as this publican.[12] I fast twice in the week, I give tithes of all that I possess.

[13] And the publican, standing afar off, would not lift up so much as his eyes unto heaven, but smote upon his breast, saying, God be merciful to me a sinner.[14] I tell you, this man went down to his house justified rather than the other: for every one that exalteth himself shall be abased; and he that humbleth himself shall be exalted.

SUMMARY

The Parable of the Pharisee and Tax Collector is a story Jesus told about two men who went to the temple to pray. One was a Pharisee (a religious leader), and the other was a tax collector, who was not liked by many people. The Pharisee prayed about how good and religious he was, while the tax collector humbly asked for God's forgiveness. Jesus said that the tax collector was the one who went home justified before God, not the Pharisee.

INTERPRETATION

The traditional meaning of this parable is that being humble and admitting our mistakes is better than being proud and thinking we're perfect. God wants us to recognize our faults and ask for His forgiveness, just like the tax collector did.

An additional insight is that it teaches us not to judge others based on their appearance or position. The Pharisee seemed like a religious and important person, but his prayer was not sincere. On the other hand, the tax collector, who many people didn't like, was the one with a humble and honest heart. This story reminds us that it's important to look deeper than the surface and to treat everyone with kindness and understanding, regardless of their status.

PERSONAL THOUGHTS

The lesson of this parable—to be humble and admit our mistakes—has been demonstrated by many successful people. Nelson Mandela, Warren Buffett, Winston Churchill, John F. Kennedy, and many others famously admitted their mistakes publicly and continued on to great successes. In my business life, I've observed that people who are humble and admit their mistakes are much more likely to receive valuable input from others, benefiting them in the long run. This parable reminds us that humility not only fosters personal growth but also builds stronger relationships and trust with those around us.

32. Parable of the Leaven, Luke 13 20-21

And again he said, Whereunto shall I liken the kingdom of God?
[21] It is like leaven, which a woman took and hid in three measures of meal, till the whole was leavened.

SUMMARY

The Parable of the Leaven is a story Jesus told about a woman who mixed a little bit of yeast into a large amount of dough. The yeast spread through the dough, making it rise and become much bigger than it was before.

INTERPRETATION

The traditional meaning of this parable is that just like the yeast makes the dough grow, a small amount of goodness or faith can spread and make a big difference in people's lives. Even if we only do a little bit, it can still create positive change.

An additional insight is that it shows how the Kingdom of God can grow and spread, even from the smallest beginnings. Just like the yeast in the dough, the message of God's love can spread throughout the world and transform lives. It reminds us to have faith in the power of small acts and trust that God can use them to create something amazing.

PERSONAL THOUGHTS

A small good deed can go a long way. In the documentary film "A Small Act," Chris Mburu, a child growing up in poverty in Kenya during a time of violence, is a prime example. Chris couldn't afford secondary school but was able to attend thanks to a donation from a Swedish woman named Hilda Back. After finishing secondary school, Chris went on to earn degrees from the University of Nairobi and Harvard Law School. He then started his own scholarship program, the Hilde Back Education Fund, which has awarded nearly 1,000 scholarships in Kenya. This story is a powerful reminder to Debbie and me of how a seemingly small act of kindness can grow into something much larger and more impactful.

33. Parable of the Pearl of Great Price – Mathew 13 45-46

Again, the kingdom of heaven is like unto a merchant man, seeking goodly pearls:
⁴⁶ Who, when he had found one pearl of great price, went and sold all that he had, and bought it.

SUMMARY

The Parable of the Pearl of Great Price is about a merchant who was looking for valuable pearls. When he found one very special, priceless pearl, he sold everything he had just to buy that one pearl because it was worth more than anything else.

INTERPRETATION

The traditional meaning of this parable is that the Kingdom of God is like the priceless pearl. When we discover how amazing it is, we should be willing to give up everything else to be part of it because it's more valuable than anything we could ever own.

An additional insight is that it teaches us to recognize the true value of our relationship with God. Just like the merchant who found the precious pearl, we should be willing to make sacrifices and let go of things that might hold us back to fully embrace the joy and peace that come from being close to God.

PERSONAL THOUGHTS

Debbie and I see this parable as a reminder to recognize and pursue what is most valuable in our lives. It could be a lifelong dream, an ambition, or a deep-seated passion, much like the pearl in the story. One of our sons had a busy and exciting life through his mid-30s. He worked as a paramedic, a scientist, an engineer, and even became the co-host of a popular TV show. Ultimately, he decided to drop everything and move to a Caribbean island, where he could be himself, enjoying the company of people who live in the moment and are extraordinarily kind and supportive. This parable teaches the importance of identifying what is truly meaningful to us and committing wholeheartedly to it. When we find something—or someone—that resonates deeply with us, the sacrifices we make are worthwhile, and our efforts are justified in the pursuit of that invaluable 'pearl' in our lives.

34. PARABLE OF THE NEW WINE IN OLD WINESKINS – MARK 2 22

And no man putteth new wine into old bottles: else the new wine doth burst the bottles, and the wine is spilled, and the bottles will be marred: but new wine must be put into new bottles.

SUMMARY

The Parable of the New Wine in Old Wineskins is a story Jesus told about putting new wine into old wineskins. In those days, people used animal skins to hold wine. When you put new wine in old wineskins, the new wine would expand as it ferments, causing the old wineskins to break, and the wine would spill out and be wasted.

INTERPRETATION

The traditional meaning of this parable is that new ideas and beliefs don't always fit well with old ways of thinking. Jesus was teaching that His message of love and forgiveness was like new wine that needed new wineskins, which meant a new way of understanding and living out their faith.

An additional insight is that it teaches us about being open to change and growth. Just like new wine needs new wineskins, we need to be willing to adapt and grow to fully embrace new ideas and experiences. This story reminds us not to cling to old ways of thinking or outdated beliefs, but to be open to learning and growing as individuals and as a community.

PERSONAL THOUGHTS

Throughout history, practices now acknowledged as profoundly unjust were once considered normal, accepted broadly and often without hesitation—even among those who were earnest in their faith. Slavery was woven into daily life, the denial of women's right to vote went unquestioned, segregation was widely enforced, and interracial marriages were shunned. These norms, though now clearly seen as morally and ethically wrong, were once part of the cultural landscape and rarely challenged by society at large.

The Parable of the New Wine in Old Wineskins encourages us to recognize that as our understanding deepens, old frameworks can be questioned with new insights. A willingness to let go of beliefs that no longer reflect compassion, justice, and empathy allows us to live more fully in the spirit of Jesus' message— open to change, growth, and a more loving approach to one another.

35. Parable of the House Built on the Rock and Sand – Mathew 7 24-27

Therefore whosoever heareth these sayings of mine, and doeth them, I will liken him unto a wise man, which built his house upon a rock:

²⁵ And the rain descended, and the floods came, and the winds blew, and beat upon that house; and it fell not: for it was founded upon a rock.

²⁶ And every one that heareth these sayings of mine, and doeth them not, shall be likened unto a foolish man, which built his house upon the sand:

²⁷ And the rain descended, and the floods came, and the winds blew, and beat upon that house; and it fell: and great was the fall of it.

SUMMARY

The Parable of the House Built on Rock and Sand is a story Jesus told about two people who built houses. One person built their house on solid rock, and the other built theirs on soft sand. When a big storm came, the house built on rock stayed strong, but the house built on sand fell because it didn't have a strong foundation.

INTERPRETATION

The traditional meaning of this parable is that we should build our lives on a strong religious foundation, which is following Jesus' teachings and being good people. If we do that, we'll be able to face the challenges and storms in our lives without falling apart.

An additional insight is that it teaches us about the importance of making wise choices and having strong character. Just like the house built on rock, we need to build our lives on values like kindness, honesty, and responsibility so that we can stand strong even when things get tough. This story reminds us the choices we make and the values we live by determine how well we can handle the challenges that come our way.

PERSONAL THOUGHTS

I was taught by my parents to prioritize fairness, honesty, and following through on promises. Of course, like everyone, I have not been perfect at that. Now, being older, it's not uncommon for me to look back on my life experiences. I find enormous contentment and happiness in memories where I sacrificed for those good values. No material goods provide the happiness of that knowledge and those memories. This parable reminds us that building our lives on solid principles, like a house on rock, leads to lasting fulfillment, far beyond what any material possessions can offer.

36. Parable of the Servant's Duty – Luke 17 7-10

But which of you, having a servant plowing or feeding cattle, will say unto him by and by, when he is come from the field, Go and sit down to meat?

⁸ And will not rather say unto him, Make ready wherewith I may sup, and gird thyself, and serve me, till I have eaten and drunken; and afterward thou shalt eat and drink?

⁹ Doth he thank that servant because he did the things that were commanded him? I trow not.

¹⁰ So likewise ye, when ye shall have done all those things which are commanded you, say, We are unprofitable servants: we have done that which was our duty to do.

SUMMARY

The Parable of the Servant's Duty is a story Jesus told about a servant who worked all day in the fields. When the servant came home, his master didn't say, "Great job! Now take a break." Instead, the master asked the servant to serve him dinner first. Jesus said that the servant should not expect a special reward for doing his job, because he was just doing what he was supposed to do.

INTERPRETATION

The traditional meaning of this parable is that we should do our best and fulfill our responsibilities and duties in service of God without expecting extra praise or rewards. Just like the servant, we should do what's right because it's our duty, not because we want something in return.

An additional insight is that it teaches us about the importance of having a humble attitude and a strong work ethic. We should focus on doing our best and serving others without seeking recognition or rewards. This story reminds us that true greatness comes from being humble, resolute, and selfless in our actions and attitudes.

PERSONAL THOUGHTS

As a young parent, Debbie read many parenting books. One common theme was to regularly compliment your kids on their accomplishments and jobs well done to help build their self-esteem. Over time, I came to question whether too much positive reinforcement diluted the importance of my words. Our children knew whether they did a good job or not, and they knew I knew as well. My words alone didn't mean a lot to them. As they grew older, I chose to both compliment and criticize less, opting for minor confirmations like a small nod of the head unless it was something very extraordinary. I honestly don't know which approach is best, and as parents, we never know if we are doing a good job, but we try our best. This parable reminds us that our duty is to do our best, even when the results are uncertain and there is no reward.

37. Parable of The Fig Tree – Mark 13 28-31

Now learn a parable of the fig tree; When her branch is yet tender, and putteth forth leaves, ye know that summer is near:

29 So ye in like manner, when ye shall see these things come to pass, know that it is nigh, even at the doors.

30 Verily I say unto you, that this generation shall not pass, till all these things be done.

31 Heaven and earth shall pass away: but my words shall not pass away.

SUMMARY

In this parable, Jesus uses the fig tree as an illustration. Just as the tender branches and new leaves of a fig tree indicate that summer is near, so too should certain events signal to us that significant changes or the fulfillment of prophecy are approaching. Jesus emphasizes that these signs are reliable like the growth of a fig tree, and His words and promises will endure forever.

INTERPRETATION

The traditional meaning of this parable is as a metaphor for the certainty and enduring truth of Jesus' teachings. Just as the fig tree's new leaves signal the inevitable arrival of summer, Jesus' words offer timeless guidance and assurance, reminding us that despite changes and challenges in life, His teachings remain a constant source of strength and direction."

An additional insight is the parable encourages patience and faith in the process of growth and renewal. Just as the fig tree does not bear leaves immediately but waits for the right season, individuals too may go through periods of apparent dormancy, only to emerge stronger and more vibrant. This teaches us to be patient and supportive of ourselves and others throughout all our periods of personal development.

PERSONAL THOUGHTS

When faced with a life challenge, Debbie says "It will all be okay in the end, if it's not okay, it's not the end". Debbie's words and this Parable remind me that life is full of ups and downs. Just as the fig tree goes through cycles of losing its leaves and then budding again, we too experience seasons of challenge and triumph. I've seen over time when facing difficulties, I should remind myself these hardships are temporary and, with time, I can overcome them. Similarly, the highs and joys of life are precious but also transient, and we should savor them in the moment but not become attached. This perspective helps us navigate life's journey with resilience and grace, knowing that both the good and the bad times are part of our growth and experience. By maintaining a steady heart and mind, we can find peace and strength in every season of life.

38. Parable of The Two Debtors – Luke 7 41-43

There was a certain creditor which had two debtors: the one owed five hundred pence, and the other fifty.

42 And when they had nothing to pay, he frankly forgave them both. Tell me therefore, which of them will love him most?

43 Simon answered and said, I suppose that he, to whom he forgave most. And he said unto him, Thou hast rightly judged.

SUMMARY

The Parable of the Two Debtors is a story Jesus told about two people who owed money to a money-lender. One owed a lot of money, the other just a little. The moneylender forgave both of their debts. Jesus then asked which person would be more grateful. The answer was the person who owed more money because they were forgiven for a bigger debt.

INTERPRETATION

The traditional meaning of this parable is when we realize how much God has forgiven us, we will be more grateful and loving. The person who was forgiven more showed greater appreciation, illustrating that those who recognize the depth of their sins and the extent of God's forgiveness will have an easier path toward love and gratitude towards God.

An additional insight is that it teaches us the power of forgiveness and its transformative effect on relationships. Being forgiven helps us be more forgiving and compassionate. This story reminds us to be grateful for forgiveness and to extend it to others.

PERSONAL THOUGHTS

As a manager some years ago, I was promoted and asked to choose who would replace me between two candidates. After my decision, the wife of the person not chosen became angry and resentful, and she spread lies and negative stories about my wife. Debbie found out and chose to forgive and still treat her with the same respect and kindness as always. Over time, the woman began to feel guilty and confessed to her Sunday school group that the stories were lies, and she apologized to Debbie. It was clearly a turning point in the woman's life.

This experience resonates deeply with the Parable of the Two Debtors. Just as the debtor who owed more was more grateful for the forgiveness, the woman's eventual remorse and apology were profound because of Debbie's unexpected and gracious forgiveness. It taught me that extending forgiveness, even when it is difficult, can lead to transformation and healing. My wife's response not only exemplified the power of forgiveness but also demonstrated how such acts can inspire significant change in others, reminding us that forgiveness is a gift that can lead to redemption and a new beginning.

39. Parable of The Vine and Branches

I am the true vine, and my Father is the husbandman.

² Every branch in me that beareth not fruit he taketh away: and every branch that beareth fruit, he purgeth it, that it may bring forth more fruit.

³ Now ye are clean through the word which I have spoken unto you.⁴ Abide in me, and I in you. As the branch cannot bear fruit of itself, except it abide in the vine; no more can ye, except ye abide in me.

⁵ I am the vine, ye are the branches: He that abideth in me, and I in him, the same bringeth forth much fruit: for without me ye can do nothing.⁶ If a man abide not in me, he is cast forth as a branch, and is withered; and men gather them, and cast them into the fire, and they are burned.

⁷ If ye abide in me, and my words abide in you, ye shall ask what ye will, and it shall be done unto you.⁸ Herein is my Father glorified, that ye bear much fruit; so shall ye be my disciples.

SUMMARY

The Parable of the Vine and the Branches is a story Jesus told about a grapevine and its branches. In a grape orchard, the main plant is a vine and it has small branches or shoots growing from it. He said that He is like the vine, and we are like the branches. Just like branches need to stay connected to the vine to grow and produce fruit, we need to stay connected to Jesus to grow and be able to do good things in our lives.

INTERPRETATION

The traditional meaning of this parable is that we need to have a close relationship with Jesus to be strong and successful in our lives. If we stay connected to Jesus through prayer, like the branches stay connected to the vine, we will be able to do great things and have a meaningful and happy life.

An additional insight is that it teaches us about the importance of relying on Jesus and others for guidance and support. We can't do everything on our own, and just like the branches need the vine to survive, we need the support of others to help us grow and become the best version of ourselves. This story reminds us that having a strong connection to Jesus, family and friends will help us in all aspects of our lives helping to succeed in making a positive impact on the world around us.

PERSONAL THOUGHTS

Jesus and our religious beliefs can offer comfort and help us when we're struggling. Also having close friends or a significant other can also provide great support and comfort. Debbie and I discuss every big decision together and make sure we both fully agree before moving forward. This has given me a lot of confidence and strength in many things I've done. In writing this book, I know no matter what happens or what people say, Debbie will find a way to see the positive side and reassure me that it was worth the effort. That's something you can't put a price on. This parable reminds us that just as branches thrive when connected to the vine, we also flourish when we are connected to supportive and loving relationships.

40. The Parable of the Rich Young Ruler – Mathew 19 16-30

And, behold, one came and said unto him, Good Master, what good thing shall I do, that I may have eternal life?

[17] And he said unto him, Why callest thou me good? there is none good but one, that is, God: but if thou wilt enter into life, keep the commandments. [18] He saith unto him, Which? Jesus said, Thou shalt do no murder, Thou shalt not commit adultery, Thou shalt not steal, Thou shalt not bear false witness,

[19] Honour thy father and thy mother: and, Thou shalt love thy neighbour as thyself. [20] The young man saith unto him, All these things have I kept from my youth up: what lack I yet?

[21] Jesus said unto him, If thou wilt be perfect, go and sell that thou hast, and give to the poor, and thou shalt have treasure in heaven: and come and follow me. [22] But when the young man heard that saying, he went away sorrowful: for he had great possessions.

[23] Then said Jesus unto his disciples, Verily I say unto you, That a rich man shall hardly enter into the kingdom of heaven. [24] And again I say unto you, It is easier for a camel to go through the eye of a needle, than for a rich man to enter into the kingdom of God.

[25] When his disciples heard it, they were exceedingly amazed, saying, Who then can be saved? [26] But Jesus beheld them, and said unto them, With men this is impossible; but with God all things are possible.

[27] Then answered Peter and said unto him, Behold, we have forsaken all, and followed thee; what shall we have therefore? [28] And Jesus said unto them, Verily I say unto you, That ye which have followed me in the regeneration, when the Son of man shall sit in the throne of his glory, ye also shall sit upon twelve thrones, judging the twelve tribes of Israel.

[29] And every one that hath forsaken houses, or brethren, or sisters, or father, or mother, or wife, or children, or lands, for my name›s sake, shall receive an hundredfold, and shall inherit everlasting life. [30] But many that are first shall be last; and the last shall be first.

SUMMARY

The Parable of the Rich Young Ruler is about a rich young man who asks Jesus what he needs to do to have eternal life. Jesus tells him to follow the commandments, but the young man says he already does that. Then Jesus tells him to sell everything he owns, give the money to the poor, and follow Jesus. The young man becomes sad because he's very wealthy and doesn't want to give up his riches.

INTERPRETATION

The traditional meaning of this parable is that it can be hard for people who love their wealth to enter the kingdom of heaven. Sometimes, we need to let go of things we love to follow God and receive eternal life.

An additional insight is that it teaches that being a good person needs to take priority in our life. We should not let our possessions or money become more important than honesty, integrity and being a good friend and family member.

PERSONAL THOUGHTS

As I've grown older, I've come to realize there are many things in life that hold more value than money. We recognize these things in the memories that give us comfort as we age. I cherish memories of prioritizing fairness in my business dealings, such as offering fair wages and excellent medical benefits to my employees. I recall instances of lending a helping hand to those in need by providing financial assistance or affordable housing, and by staying true to honest and ethical values. These experiences have taught me that true fulfillment comes from helping others and staying true to my principles, rather than simply pursuing wealth. This parable reminds us that while wealth can provide comfort, it is our actions and values that bring lasting happiness and fulfillment.

41. PARABLE OF THE STRONG MAN – MATHEW 12 29

Or else how can one enter into a strong man's house, and spoil his goods, except he first bind the strong man? and then he will spoil his house.

SUMMARY

The Parable of the Strong Man is a story Jesus told about a strong man who protected his house. The strong man represents the devil protecting evil. If someone tried to break into the house and steal his things, they wouldn't be able to do it unless they first tied up the strong man. Once the strong man was tied up, they could easily take his belongings.

INTERPRETATION

The traditional meaning of this parable is that to overcome evil, you must first deal with its source. In the story, Jesus represents the one who ties up the strong man (the devil), so people can be set free from the devil's control and influence in their lives.

An additional insight is that it teaches us about the power of controlling negative thoughts and actions in our lives. We have the God given the power to "tie up" bad tendencies through a conscience and the power to control our thoughts and actions helping us live a better life. The story encourages us to trust our heart and our conscience to keep us on a good path away from the negative influences of the world.

PERSONAL THOUGHTS

A close friend served as CEO of a small company where my son worked. During a period of financial turmoil, my friend made the tough decision to terminate my son's employment to cut costs. Fueled by a desire for retribution, and being on the Board, I agreed to the Board's proposal to dismiss my friend, citing ongoing financial struggles as justification. I could have dissented and likely changed the mind of the Board.

In the aftermath, our friendship dissolved irreparably. Reflecting on the situation now, I realize my desire for vengeance only caused further harm. Tying up the 'devil' of vengeance, as suggested in the parable, would have been wiser. Interestingly, despite the initial setback, my son benefited from the experience, as it led to unforeseen opportunities. In the end, my own need for vengeance inflicted pain on me as well as others, while my friend's actions, though difficult, were ultimately borne out of necessity.

42. THE PARABLE OF THE WEDDING BANQUET – MATHEW 22 1-14

22 Jesus spoke to them again in parables, saying: [2] "The kingdom of heaven is like a king who prepared a wedding banquet for his son. [3] He sent his servants to those who had been invited to the banquet to tell them to come, but they refused to come.

[4] "Then he sent some more servants and said, 'Tell those who have been invited that I have prepared my dinner: My oxen and fattened cattle have been butchered, and everything is ready. Come to the wedding banquet.'

[5] "But they paid no attention and went off—one to his field, another to his business. [6] The rest seized his servants, mistreated them and killed them. [7] The king was enraged. He sent his army and destroyed those murderers and burned their city.

[8] "Then he said to his servants, 'The wedding banquet is ready, but those I invited did not deserve to come. [9] So go to the street corners and invite to the banquet anyone you find.' [10] So the servants went out into the streets and gathered all the people they could find, the bad as well as the good, and the wedding hall was filled with guests.

[11] "But when the king came in to see the guests, he noticed a man there who was not wearing wedding clothes. [12] He asked, 'How did you get in here without wedding clothes, friend?' The man was speechless.

[13] "Then the king told the attendants, 'Tie him hand and foot, and throw him outside, into the darkness, where there will be weeping and gnashing of teeth.'

[14] "For many are invited, but few are chosen."

Summary

In this parable, Jesus compares the Kingdom of Heaven to a wedding feast organized by a king for his son. The king invites guests, but they refuse to come. Even after sending multiple invitations and detailing the grand feast, the guests don't show up. Some even go so far as to mistreat and kill the servants delivering the invitations. Angry, the king orders his troops to kill those who harmed his servants and burn their city. Then, he orders his servants to invite anyone they find on the street. When the feast begins, the king notices a man without wedding clothes and orders him to be thrown out, declaring that many are invited but few are chosen.

Interpretation

The traditional meaning of this parable is it portrays the idea that God extends an invitation to humanity to join the divine Kingdom, symbolized by the wedding feast. The refusal of the first guests can be seen as an allegory for how the Israelites, God's chosen people, did not recognize the coming of the Messiah, Jesus. Their violent reaction represents the persecution of prophets and messengers sent by God, culminating in the crucifixion of Jesus. The opening of the feast to anyone, both good and bad, symbolizes the extension of God's invitation to Gentiles as well as Jews.

An additional insight is the man who is thrown out for not wearing wedding clothes symbolizes those who may answer the call to join the Kingdom of God but are not prepared or willing to live according to its principles. This underscores the notion that while the invitation is open to all, the standards of the kingdom must still be met. Being part of the Kingdom of Heaven requires more than just showing up; it requires a commitment to live according to God's laws.

Personal Thoughts

Many people live their lives guided by a great set of core values. They are kind, generous, and have a very positive attitude toward everyone and life in general. I believe people who live this type of life will not be turned away from Heaven. We all have the opportunity to live according to good values, help others, and be positive and forgiving. There is no better feeling than knowing you lived a good life.

All the best to each of you!

EPILOGUE

Moses, a central figure in the Old Testament, led the Israelites out of Egypt in the 13th century BCE and was entrusted with the divine revelation of God's laws—the Mosaic Covenant—at Mount Sinai. Centuries later, King David established the United Kingdom of Israel, which continued to uphold the laws from Moses. Then, around 600 BCE, the Prophet Jeremiah foretold a time when God would establish a New Covenant, writing His laws upon the hearts of His people—a shift signifying a deeper, more personal relationship with God.

In the Book of Jeremiah (31:31–34), God says He will make a New Covenant with the House of Israel and Judah, different from the one given when He led them out of Egypt. God says He will "write it in their hearts," declaring that from the least to the greatest, all shall know Him, and He will remember their sin no more:

"31 Behold, the days come, saith the Lord, that I will make a new covenant with the house of Israel, and with the house of Judah: 32 Not according to the covenant that I made with their fathers in the day that I took them by the hand to bring them out of the land of Egypt; which my covenant they brake, although I was an husband unto them, saith the Lord: 33 But this shall be the covenant that I will make with the house of Israel; After those days, saith the Lord, I will put my law in their inward parts, and write it in their hearts; and will be their God, and they shall be my people. 34 And they shall teach no more every man his neighbour, and every man his brother, saying, Know the Lord: for they shall all know me, from the least of them unto the greatest of them, saith the Lord: for I will forgive their iniquity, and I will remember their sin no more."

In the New Testament, Jesus embodies and fulfills this New Covenant. Through His teachings and parables, He offers renewed guidance and a deeper understanding of God's will, emphasizing love, grace, and mercy. Jesus thus provides us with the perfect role model, while His parables retain a timeless relevance and the power to transform our lives today.

When comparing the Old and New Testament, religious scholars offer varied perspectives on how to reconcile perceived differences. My personal belief is that wherever we see distinctions in rules or practices, we should follow the guidance and role modeling of Jesus in the New Testament—seeing His purpose as clarifying and elevating the older laws. Others hold different views, and there is no definitive answer, as we are all interpreting the knowledge and guidance we have been given to the best of our ability.

In Matthew, the first book of the New Testament, we find a simple yet profound summary of how Jesus instructs us to live:

(Matthew   22:36–40)
"Jesus says the greatest commandments are to love God and to love your neighbor as yourself, summarizing the law and the prophets."

As we read the stories of Christ in the New Testament Gospels, we see evidence of the New Covenant foretold by Jeremiah, alongside teachings that appear to differ from the Mosaic Covenant. Below are just a few examples:

Mosaic Covenant vs. New Covenant

1. **Eye for an Eye (Exodus 21:24) vs. Turn the Other Cheek (Matthew 5:38–39)**

   - *Exodus:* "Eye for eye, tooth for tooth, hand for hand, foot for foot."
   - *Matthew:* Jesus teaches non-retaliation and an ethic of mercy. "Ye have heard that it hath been said, An eye for an eye, and a tooth for a tooth: But I say unto you, That ye resist not evil: but whosoever shall smite thee on thy right cheek, turn to him the other also."

2. **Punishment for Adultery (Leviticus 20:10) vs. The Woman Caught in Adultery (John 8:1–11)**

   - *Leviticus:* Calls for death to both the adulterer and adulteress. "If a man commits adultery with another man's wife—even with the wife of his neighbor—both the adulterer and the adulteress are to be put to death."
   - *John:* Jesus shows mercy and instructs the woman to go, and sin no more. "Let him who is without sin among you be the first to throw a stone at her." Eventually, all accusers leave, and Jesus tells the woman, "Neither do I condemn you: go, and from now on sin no more."

3. **Capital Punishment for Blasphemy (Leviticus 24:16) vs. Forgive Seventy-Times-Seven (Matthew 18:21–22)**

   - *Leviticus:* Calls for stoning "And he that blasphemeth the name of the Lord, he shall surely be put to death, and all the congregation shall certainly stone him: as well the stranger, as he that is born in the land, when he blasphemeth the name of the Lord, shall be put to death."
   - *Matthew:* Jesus underscores limitless forgiveness. "Then came Peter to him, and said, Lord, how oft shall my brother sin against me, and I forgive him? till seven times? 22 Jesus saith unto him, I say not unto thee, Until seven times: but, Until seventy times seven."

4. **Love Your Enemies (Matthew 5:43-44)**

   - "Ye have heard that it hath been said, Thou shalt love thy neighbour, and hate thine enemy. But I say unto you, Love your enemies, bless them that curse you, do good to them that hate you, and pray for them which despitefully use you, and persecute you."

Further Reading: Bridging the Old and New

For those seeking to explore how the early Christians wrestled with the transition from Mosaic laws to the New Covenant, **Hebrews 8–10** offers a thorough theological perspective. These chapters discuss the concept of Jesus as the ultimate High Priest and the final, perfect sacrifice, thereby rendering some of the old sacrificial rules unnecessary. By comparing Jesus' priesthood to the Levitical system, the author of Hebrews underscores a shift from an external system of rituals toward an internalized faith, aligning with Jeremiah's prophecy of God's law being "written on our hearts."

Additionally, **Acts 15** recounts a pivotal moment in the early Church—often called the Council of Jerusalem—where the apostles and elders deliberate on whether Gentile converts must adhere to certain Mosaic regulations (such as circumcision). Their decision to focus on core tenets of faith and behavior rather than comprehensive adherence to all older laws exemplifies how believers navigated these shifting covenantal boundaries. This passage reflects the Church's aim to honor its Jewish roots while embracing a broader, more inclusive application of Jesus' teachings.

While these ancient debates and epistles might seem distant from our 21st-century challenges, the core themes remain highly relevant. Embracing the New Covenant means emphasizing **love, mercy, and spiritual transformation** over strict rule-keeping or external rituals. Today, we can practice this by:

- **Showing Grace:** Rather than seeking retribution or holding grudges, we follow Jesus' model of forgiveness and reconciliation.
- **Practicing Compassion:** We can mirror Jesus' concern for the marginalized, ensuring that our local communities receive empathy and tangible support.
- **Rethinking Retribution:** Instead of insisting on punitive measures, we might advocate restorative approaches that focus on healing and betterment for all involved.
- **Engaging in Intentional Spiritual Growth:** Through prayer, study, and reflection on Jesus' words, we cultivate an inward faith that genuinely transforms our daily actions and relationships.

In essence, applying the New Covenant approach to modern life challenges us to invite the Holy Spirit to shape our hearts, so our motivations and choices flow from sincere love for God and for others—our life can be a living testimony of the grace and moral excellence Jesus taught through His parables. We have been shown a path of compassion, spiritual insight, and a willingness to evolve our understanding of God's intent. Whether you approach these teachings as a Christian seeking deeper faith or as someone looking for universal ethical guidance, the message of Jesus invites transformation, empathy, and renewal.

ABOUT THE AUTHOR

Richard Louden's journey as a seeker of spiritual wisdom was profoundly shaped by The Gospels of Jesus in the Christian faith. With a diverse background as an entrepreneur enriched by experiences living overseas, exploring different cultures, extensive travel, and the joys and challenges of family life, he has long been drawn to the insights of Christian teachings, seeking ways to merge Christianity and religion with the practicalities of personal and professional life.

The book finds its roots in a deep enduring appreciation of the Parables of the Gospels and a period of profound personal trial. Long before life's toughest tests, Richard and his wife, Debbie, turned to these parables for guidance and comfort. However, when Debbie received a diagnosis of an aggressive form of endometrial cancer, the Parables took on an even deeper, more urgent meaning in their lives. Amid the physically and emotionally draining journey of chemotherapy, radiation, and immunotherapy, researching these stories became more than an academic exercise—it became a lifeline. These teachings offered hope, understanding, and resilience, bringing comfort to both Richard and Debbie through the most challenging of times.

Richard's approach to the Gospels is that of an earnest seeker—a person who looks beyond the surface to uncover universal truths relevant to modern life. His interpretations, grounded in real-world experiences, aim to resonate with readers from diverse backgrounds, offering relatable insights drawn from his own life journey.

Today, as Debbie faces a relapse and the spread of her cancer, this book stands as a tribute to their shared journey through adversity, fortified by the timeless wisdom of the Parables. Richard invites readers to walk alongside him in exploring these age-old teachings, viewed through the lens of everyday struggles and victories, with the hope that they too might find solace, strength, and guidance in the Parables.

References
and
Supplementary Reading

Bailey, Kenneth E. *Jesus Through Middle Eastern Eyes: Cultural Studies in the Gospels*. Downers Grove, IL: IVP Academic, 2008.

Boice, James Montgomery. *The Parables of Jesus: Lessons in Life from the Master Teacher*. Chicago: Moody Publishers, 1983.

Capon, Robert Farrar. *Kingdom, Grace, Judgment: Paradox, Outrage, and Vindication in the Parables of Jesus*. Grand Rapids, MI: Eerdmans, 2002.

Crossan, John Dominic. *The Historical Jesus: The Life of a Mediterranean Jewish Peasant*. San Francisco: HarperSanFrancisco, 1991.

Dodd, C.H. *Parables of the Kingdom*. New York: Charles Scribner's Sons, 1st edition, 1961.

Edersheim, Alfred. *The Life and Times of Jesus the Messiah*. Peabody, MA: Hendrickson Publishers, 1993.

Gaebelein, Frank E., ed. *The Expositor's Bible Commentary*. Grand Rapids, MI: Zondervan, 1976-1992.

Hultgren, Arland J. *The Parables of Jesus: A Commentary*. Grand Rapids, MI: Eerdmans, 2000.

Jeremias, Joachim. *The Parables of Jesus*. New York: Charles Scribner's Sons, 1963.

Mitchell, Stephen. *The Gospel According to Jesus: A New Translation and Guide to His Essential Teachings for Believers and Unbelievers*. New York: HarperCollins, 1991.

Snodgrass, Klyne R. *Stories with Intent: A Comprehensive Guide to the Parables of Jesus*. Grand Rapids, MI: Eerdmans, 2008.

Wright, N.T. *Jesus and the Victory of God*. Minneapolis: Fortress Press, 1996.

Wright, N.T. *The New Testament and the People of God*. Minneapolis: Fortress Press, 1992.

Young, Brad H. *The Parables: Jewish Tradition and Christian Interpretation*. Peabody, MA: Hendrickson Publishers, 1998.

Commentary Series

The Anchor Yale Bible Commentary Series. Various authors. New Haven, CT: Yale University Press.

The Interpretation Commentary Series. Various authors. Louisville, KY: Westminster John Knox Press.

The New International Commentary on the New Testament (NICNT). Various authors. Grand Rapids, MI: Eerdmans.

The Word Biblical Commentary (WBC). Various authors. Grand Rapids, MI: Zondervan.

Journals

Catholic Biblical Quarterly. Washington, D.C.: Catholic Biblical Association of America.

Journal for the Study of the New Testament. London: SAGE Publications.

Journal of Biblical Literature. Atlanta: Society of Biblical Literature.

New Testament Studies. Cambridge: Cambridge University Press.

Online Resources

Bible Gateway. Available at: https://www.biblegateway.com

BibleHub. Available at: https://biblehub.com

Blue Letter Bible. Available at: https://www.blueletterbible.org